BEST OF BRITISH

———————————— ⌒⌒ ————————————

JON HENDERSON has been a sports journalist for forty years. A former Reuters correspondent, he has reported on five Olympics, countless England cricket tours and two football World Cups, and he has covered every Wimbledon since 1969. He is now tennis correspondent and associate sports editor of the *Observer*.

MARK THOMAS is an award-winning illustrator. Over the past three decades his career has covered television, film, advertising and publishing. He lives in Surrey with his wife and daughters.

To Charlie, who died aged twenty-two as a result of diabetes

He strode with gaiety and courage, contemptuous of care,
along the narrow crumbling ridge from which he sensed
he must inevitably fall, towards the castle of his hopes.
We watched with fearful admiration.

JAMES HENDERSON

The author is donating his proceeds from this book to the
Juvenile Diabetes Research Foundation
(www.jdrf.org.uk).

JON HENDERSON

BEST OF BRITISH
HENDO'S SPORTING HEROES

ILLUSTRATIONS BY MARK THOMAS

YELLOW JERSEY PRESS

LONDON

Published by Yellow Jersey Press 2007

2 4 6 8 10 9 7 5 3 1

Copyright © Jon Henderson 2007

Jon Henderson has asserted his right under the Copyright, Designs
and Patents Act 1988 to be identified as the author of this work

First published in Great Britain in 2007 by
Yellow Jersey Press

Random House, 20 Vauxhall Bridge Road,
London SW1V 2SA

www.rbooks.co.uk

Addresses for companies within The Random House Group Limited
can be found at: www.randomhouse.co.uk/offices.htm

The Random House Group Limited Reg. No. 954009

A CIP catalogue record for this book
is available from the British Library

ISBN 9780224082488

The Random House Group Limited makes every effort to ensure that
the papers used in its books are made from trees that have been legally
sourced from well-managed and credibly certified forests. Our paper
procurement policy can be found at: www.rbooks.co.uk/environment

Set in 11 on 14pt Dante
Designed by Peter Ward
Printed and bound in Germany by
GGP Media GmbH, Pößneck

CONTENTS

INTRODUCTION

Friends of a cynical disposition thought it must have been a struggle to find 100 British sporting heroes. Not a bit of it. The difficulties I faced keeping the entries to that figure gave me a mild sense of guilt that at times during my journalistic career I might have been overly harsh on selectors. I did not even have to rely on heroes from the days when we Brits were unchallenged on the games field, the time when we were starting it all by 'frivolling at garden parties' – to quote Lottie Dod of these pages only slightly out of context – while the rest of the world was still being serious. We have never been short of sporting heroes, including today when we anguish over our failures and forget that sport's universality has inevitably diminished our share of champions. As I put the finishing touches to this volume, there are already impressive candidates for an updated version – cyclist Nicole Cooke, motor racer Lewis Hamilton, rowing's Andy Hodge, boxer Amir Khan, tennis player Andy Murray, football's Wayne Rooney and athlete Nicola Sanders, to name just a few. A far harder task than choosing the heroes – 102, in fact, as two combinations, the golfing Morrises and the ice skaters Torvill and Dean, are each counted as one – was the casting aside. David Beckham, Tom Finney, Geoff Hurst, Len Hutton, Ann Packer, Paula Radcliffe and Virginia Wade are among those who almost persuaded me to go for a greater number. Some of you may find it difficult to reconcile certain exclusions with those who have been chosen, but candidates were assessed not only on what they achieved but what they achieved in relation to considerations such as opportunity, physical attributes and, given the title of this book, whether there was an heroic element. Several ways of ordering the heroes, drawn from Northern Ireland as well as the British mainland, would have made sense. Chronologically by date of birth seemed the best, although I have listed those born in the same year alphabetically. This way, when read from start to finish, the book has an historical narrative. Reader or dipper, you are welcome to this distillation of my lifetime's interest, which has kept me occupied over more than four decades while on the lookout for a proper job.

JON HENDERSON, July 2007

ROBIN HOOD

PART ONE

OUT OF THE GREENWOOD
1377–1764

ROBIN HOOD
EARLIEST MENTION, C.1377

ROBIN HOOD's name first crops up in *Piers Plowman*, written in or about 1377 – and more than six hundred years on the fabled figure is still with us, complete with lip-glossed squeeze Maid Marian, as a star of the big screen. The *Encyclopaedia Britannica* addresses, with due solemnity, the question of whether there is any truth in the legend. 'For our part,' it concludes in a lengthy essay, 'we are not disinclined to believe that the Robin Hood story has some historical basis, however fanciful and romantic the superstructure . . . He is the great sportsman, the incomparable archer, the lover of the green-wood and of a free life, brave, adventurous, jocular, open-handed, a protector of women.' This being so far removed from the lurid world of the twenty-first-century Premiership footballer should do nothing to diminish his claim to a place in the history of sport. Through the stories of Robin Hood we glimpse the first recognisable forms of modern sports, adapted from deadly martial pursuits such as archery and sword fighting. Municipal ranges were common across England after Edward III made archery practice compulsory in 1363, and deciding who could shoot farthest or straightest would have been as natural as setting fire to the village witch. Similarly, a way of determining the finest swordsmen that did not involve corpses almost certainly developed from fencing demonstrations at fairs and in market places. Robin Hood's ability as a bowman is a persistent theme of the legend, with two stories in particular recurring. One involves a 'proud potter' who beats Robin in a fight. The pair become friends and exchange clothing so that Robin can go in disguise to Nottingham. Here he arouses the interest of the sheriff, a frequent victim of Robin's wealth-redistribution schemes, by performing brilliantly in an archery contest. Still impersonating the potter, Robin tricks the sheriff into going to the forest where he is relieved of his horse and other possessions. The second story is of the silver arrow contest outside the walls of Nottingham. A huge crowd watch the field being reduced to two: Robin and Gilbert with the White Hand, the sheriff's stooge. For the shoot-off, a willow wand replaces the target. Robin goes first and splits it; Gilbert misses. The presentation ceremony turns into a riot when Robin goes forward to accept the prize: an arrow with a silver tip and shaft. The sheriff, reneging on his promise to behave honourably, orders him to be seized. Robin fights his way free and escapes. Centuries later, archery becomes an Olympic sport.

HENRY VIII
1491–1547

HENRY VIII's competitive drive, a characteristic of ambitious second sons, showed no sign of diminishing when his older brother, Arthur, died in 1502. Henry was still ten at the time; seven years later on the death of his father, Henry VII, he was crowned king. The responsibilities of leading a nation with an expanding foreign policy, the distraction of internal strife caused by the Reformation and the demands of a complicated private life could not quell Henry's lust for action. This paragon of princes, as robust as Arthur had been sickly,

4

sought other outlets – and in finding them laid claim to being the first and greatest of all-round sportsmen. He could bend a bow with the best foresters in the land, matching them at shooting at the butts (targets) and flight shooting (distance). He was a champion at tennis – seeing him play was 'the prettiest thing in the world' in the view of the Venetian ambassador to London – and a jouster whose immense suit of tilting armour in the Tower of London gives a hint of his prowess in the lists. The Dutch humanist and scholar Erasmus reckoned he had seen no finer thrower of a hunting dart, having seen the King kill a deer with a single hit. He was so keen on bowling that he took a 90 feet by 8 feet indoor bowling shed with him on an expedition against France. He competed impressively at two-handed sword tournaments, the use of armour and blunted swords being encouraged to restrict fatalities, and loved to wrestle. His most famous wrestling match, against Francis I at the Field of the Cloth of Gold in northern France, ended in controversy. The English camp claimed Henry was felled by an illegal 'Breton trip' and did not report it; French chronicles made much of Francis's brilliant victory. Henry employed an Italian coach to help him perfect an early version of dressage, and gave hour-long demonstrations that included many elaborate manoeuvres, climaxing with a thousand jumps in the air. He had racing stables at Greenwich and Windsor and four jockeys who wore 'ryding cappes of blac veilute and 22 butons of golde to garish them'. On top of all this, he built some of the great sporting arenas of the age. His palaces at Greenwich and Whitehall included tiltyards for jousting, bowling alleys, tennis courts and cock pits.

JAMES FIGG
▸—◂ 1695–1734 ▸—◂

JAMES FIGG, the youngest of seven children born into a poor family in Oxfordshire in the late seventeenth century, was a sword and cudgel fighter, bare-knuckle pugilist and friend of royalty. His main legacy was as a fist fighter and he is regarded as the first champion boxer, having established supremacy over all his great rivals, men such as Tim Buck, Tom Stokes and Bill Flanders. In a three-instalment fight with one of his fiercest challengers, Ned Smith of Gravesend, Figg won with sword, fists and cudgel. With an element of wrestling still allowed, Figg grappled Smith to defeat in the fist fight after being flattened by a punch. His reputation established by 1719, Figg received backing from his patron, the Earl of Peterborough, to establish a school of arms on what is now Tottenham Court Road in central London. Recreational fighting was growing in popularity and the enterprise was soon a major attraction, especially for groups of noblemen who were particularly keen to find outlets for their aggression. As Figg's fame grew, the artist William Hogarth designed his business card, which introduced him as 'master of the noble science of defence'. Hogarth also put his new pugilist friend in his engravings *Rake's Progress* and *Southwark Fair*. Later, Figg built an amphitheatre to stage prizefights that attracted such large crowds that he introduced the forerunner of today's boxing ring, raised and enclosed with wooden rails. His own services as a fighter were much in demand and at Southwark Fair he fought regularly in a booth against anyone who dared to challenge him. He also defended his championship in formal contests before retiring undefeated in 1730. His standing was such that he joined the Prince of Wales's royal circle where he hobnobbed with his Highness and other blue bloods. He died leaving a large family and the general recognition of his having been 'The Father of Boxing'. His death was recorded in all the newspapers of the day, including one notice that began: 'Last Saturday there was a Trial of Skill between the unconquered Hero, Death, on the one side and the till then unconquered Hero Mr James Figg, the famous Prize-Fighter and Master of the Noble Science of Defence on the other . . .'

ECLIPSE
1764–1789

ALONE AMONG the heroes in these pages, Eclipse is included for the vigour of his seed. But he is also a candidate as an exceptional racehorse. He started racing when he was five and was unbeaten in eighteen starts between May 1769 and October 1770, his rider supposedly never having to resort to whip or spurs. He was so good that he prompted one of racing's most enduring utterances, 'Eclipse first, and the rest nowhere', from his incorrigible Irish owner, Dennis O'Kelly. In making it, O'Kelly correctly predicted that the opposition would not be credited with a place, which was the custom if a horse lost by more than a distance (240 yards) in races that were invariably four miles or more. Eclipse's ability was such that absurd claims were made on his behalf, including one that he galloped at the rate of a mile a minute. A more sober assessment was provided by the breeding expert Tom Morris, who referred to him as 'unsurpassed in achievement as athlete and progenitor'. It is in the second of these capacities that Eclipse unquestionably stands out, with proof of the provenance of his extended family beyond reproach. The markings are still there for all to see. Foaled on 1 April 1764, a day on which the moon passed between the earth and the sun, Eclipse was a chestnut with a white blaze down his face, an off hind leg that was white from the hock down and with black spots on his rump that, in particular, have survived as a certifying hallmark. Scientists from the Royal Veterinary College delved deeper. In 2005, they reconstructed one of Eclipse's legs to try to unlock the secret of why he was so dominant. The surprising conclusion was that he was smaller than modern racehorses. 'Rather than being some freak of nature with incredible properties,' said the man who led the study, Dr Alan Wilson, 'he was actually just right in absolutely every way.' On the breeding side, the RVC established that nearly 80 per cent of thoroughbred racehorses running today can trace their ancestry back to Eclipse in the male line and most of those that cannot have him in their pedigree. The case, therefore, is overwhelming that a large majority of the great champions are members of the Eclipse family. The entire field for the 2006 Derby was directly related, as were those for the French and Kentucky Derbys. Nor is it just champions of the flat that share a genetic path back to Eclipse. Two of the great jumping champions of the twentieth century, Arkle and Desert Orchid, had this most famous of impregnators to thank for supplying them with the wherewithal to run and leap quite so capably.

DANIEL MENDOZA

PART TWO

RULES BRITANNIA
1764–1847

DANIEL MENDOZA
━━◄ 1764–1836 ►━━

DANIEL MENDOZA was said to have changed the image of Jews in England as radically as he did the art of boxing. Proud to call himself Mendoza the Jew, his feats as a prizefighter – beating much larger men by placing skill above brute force – helped to end the stereotyping of his people as vulnerable and undeserving of respect. He was born and raised in London's East End, where he had a number of jobs, including as an actor. When he turned to prizefighting, Mendoza, who was only 5 feet 7 inches and 160 pounds, forsook the slugging and mauling style that had been popular in the sport's early days. Instead he employed a more scientific approach, which he advocated in published works such as *The Art of Boxing*. Typically, he wrote: 'If your adversary aims all round blows, which is generally the case with a man ignorant of Boxing, you should strike straight forward, as a direct line reaches its target sooner than one which is circular.' His first recorded fight was a knockout victory over Harry the Coalheaver, whom he beat in 40 rounds. He soon earned the patronage of the Prince of Wales, later George IV, and was reckoned to be the first Jew to speak to George III. Three bitter fights against Richard Humphries between 1788 and 1790 made him widely known. He lost the first, possibly as the result of Humphries's second stepping forward to block a blow, but won the other two, the third one marking the first time English spectators paid to watch a sporting event. He won the title of English champion with victories over Bill Warr in 1792 at Smitham Bottom, near Croydon, and in 1794 on Bexley Common. He lost the title to 'Gentleman' John Jackson in 1795. Jackson, who was 42 pounds heavier, employed his greater bulk and a move that was still permitted, holding an opponent's hair with one hand while hitting him with the other, to win in nine rounds. In later life, Mendoza earned a living as landlord of the Admiral Nelson in Whitechapel and, as he informed the public in a letter to *The Times* in 1807, as a teacher of his scientific method of boxing. Financial problems forced him into occasional comebacks, the last of them when he was fifty-six. He died, deeply in debt, aged seventy-two.

ROBERT BARCLAY
1779–1854

LEFT TO THEIR OWN devices, athletic types have always improvised ways to demonstrate their prowess. Perhaps the epitome of this breed was Captain Robert Barclay. He made his name in the days before games were defined by rules and when prize money and gambling had started to offer financial inducements. Barclay, who became the sixth Laird of Ury, in 1797, aged seventeen, was physically robust from childhood. One nineteenth-century chronicler described him as 'a man whose pride and pleasure it was to exhibit the physical potentialities of human nature in their highest stretch'. His father, an MP, filled him with tales of prizefighting and acts of strength and endurance from an early age. His fascination developed into a passion to be involved himself after he was sent from Scotland to school near London. Here he gained first-hand knowledge of what for him was a heady mix of games and gaming. In time, his repertoire included lifting great weights. He was credited with raising 1,176 pounds and lifting a 240-pound man in the palm of one hand. Where he really surpassed all others, though, was in speed and endurance walking – and profiting from the accompanying wagers. He was still at school when he set out to cover six miles in less than an hour. Doing this with 'fair toe and heel' contact with the ground is not easy, but young Barclay managed it comfortably to secure his 100 guineas, the surprisingly large amount sanctioned by his father. This was the start of a series of walking feats that culminated in the one that established his reputation – walking one mile every hour of every day until he had completed 1,000 miles in 1,000 hours. He accomplished this unprecedented feat in 1809 on Newmarket Heath with wagers piling up to an estimated 16,000 guineas, a colossal sum for those days. Towards the finish, the crowds swelled to such a size that the area where he walked had to be roped off. At 3.15 p.m. on the final day of an ordeal that had taken him to the very limits of his stamina, Barclay set out on the 1,000th mile. There were 45 minutes left. He finished 23 minutes inside his deadline. The crowd went wild, the church bells pealed. The walk had been meticulously planned and so was his recovery. That night he was woken at midnight for a light meal because of the perils of sleeping deeply for too long after extreme exertion. Eight days later he left Ramsgate with his regiment to fight the French. He remained supremely fit and was in his seventies when he made his host at a dinner party, 'a fully adult man of more than 12 stone', stand on his right palm before lifting him on to the table. He died after being kicked in the head while trying to break in a pony.

GEORGE BYRON
1788–1824

GEORGE BYRON, who was ten when he became sixth
Baron Byron of Rochdale in 1798, had a passion for sport
that a congenital deformity in his right leg and the obligatory
debilitating lifestyle of a romantic poet could not suppress.
The effect of his dysplasia was a leg that was abnormally thin
and a small foot, which explained why he always wore long
trousers, even when swimming. In the water, his upper-body
strength and intrepid spirit meant he could compete strongly,
particularly over longer distances. At school at Harrow, he was
also an avid cricketer and boxer. In cricket, he batted with a
runner – under later laws to qualify for one of these an injury
had to be sustained after the team was announced – but still
managed to bowl. He was the prime mover in the first Eton v.
Harrow match in 1805, which took place on the site of the
modern Dorset Square in London, where Thomas Lord had
laid out a ground that was a predecessor to his eponymous
masterpiece in St John's Wood. In Byron's own words,
Harrow 'were most confoundedly beat' – by an innings and
two runs. Byron, having contributed scores of seven and two,
took off afterwards with the players of both teams to the West
End to 'kick up a convivial row in the Haymarket Theatre'.
Byron's interest in boxing sprang from the bullying he had
suffered at Harrow. This led to staged contests between the
bullies and the bullied in which Byron, only 5 feet 8 inches but
with a long reach, lost 'but one battle out of seven'. He took
his boxing so seriously that he sparred with England's prize-
ring champion 'Gentleman' John Jackson at a time when
sparring was almost as full-blooded as the real thing. At

Cambridge, Byron largely ignored his studies in favour of swimming, shooting pistols and playing cricket. Swimming was his greatest love and his feats of endurance in the water made long-distance swimming fashionable before it became an established sport. He swam across the mouth of the Tagus river at Lisbon and from the Lido to the Rialto Bridge in Venice. In an age before more scientific methods took over, he warmed up for and recovered from his four-hour Venetian swim by having sex. The exploit for which he is best known was crossing the Hellespont (Dardanelles) between Greece and Turkey in May 1810, a swim, allowing for drift, of some four miles. He failed in his first attempt with Lieutenant Ekenhead, a member of the crew of the *Salsette*, on which he was travelling. The pair were pulled from the water so numb and exhausted from battling the currents they could not stand. Two weeks later they were successful. Byron took 70 minutes, Ekenhead five minutes less, to become the first to prove that Leander's swim across the Hellespont to his inamorata Hero, a story enshrined in Greek mythology, was possible.

WILLIAM WEBB ELLIS
1806–1872

WILLIAM WEBB ELLIS was the schoolboy who by showing 'a fine disregard for the rules of football as played in his time' is credited with having invented rugby. This quotation is taken from the headstone erected in the Rugby School grounds in Ellis's honour, but it is worth noting that the plaque was not unveiled until 1 November 1923. This was one hundred years after Ellis was supposed to have scooped up the ball in his arms in defiance of the so-called rules of football, which existed only on an ad hoc basis at the time. In 1823, games at public schools were mostly free-time activities of the pupils' own devising and running with the ball in hand may not have been that unusual. It seems Ellis was singled out as the inventor of rugby on the say-so of an Old Rugbeian named Matthew Bloxam. He had left the school before 1820 but still felt qualified to give a vivid account of Ellis's moment of improvisation that would have such a profound effect over the next 200 years, particularly on the lives of New Zealanders. Later, another Old Rugbeian, Thomas Hughes, who wrote the classic *Tom Brown's Schooldays*, cast doubt on whether Ellis would have run with the ball. In 1897, he wrote a letter to a sub-committee of the OR Society that was examining the origin of the game. In it he said that in his first year, 1834, running with the ball in hand was absolutely forbidden and if anyone had been killed doing it the verdict would almost certainly have been 'justifiable homicide'. Hughes said that carrying the ball was popularised in 1838–9 by a fast, thickset boy called Jem Mackie. The debate over Ellis would never have taken place if rugby, like the variations of football conceived at other public schools – notably Eton and Winchester – had stayed within the school grounds. That it spread is usually ascribed to Dr Thomas Arnold. Arnold, who was at Rugby School from 1828 to 1842, was very possibly the most influential headmaster there has ever been. Even though he was not himself actively involved with games, he accepted their worth and occasionally appeared on the touchline. This was enough for those devoted members of his staff who went on to be headmasters elsewhere to spread the gospel of games played at Rugby, including the creation for which Ellis now takes credit. It will never be known for sure whether Ellis, who went on to become a priest, did have a role in initiating rugby. He stands rather as the symbolic champion of all those public-school masters and boys in the nineteenth century whose energetic afternoons produced games that are now watched and played by millions.

ALFRED MYNN
⟜ 1807–1861 ⟝

ALFRED MYNN was the Falstaffian frontiersman of cricket whose exploits in the first half of the nineteenth century accelerated the game's popularity. He was the 'Lion of Kent', a hop farmer and man of extreme size whose boots, it was said, were too big for all but W. G. Grace to fill.

'Beef and beer are the things to play cricket on,' was a Mynn dictum that he observed heartily. At more than 6 feet and weighing as much as 24 stone, according to some reports, he was a mighty presence on the cricket field even before he catapulted down his round-arm deliveries off a five-stride run. This was a time of transition in cricket – between the eras of underarm and overarm (legalised in 1864) when round-arm enabled bowlers to generate far greater pace on pitches that were nowhere near as flat as they are now. As a consequence the balance tipped conclusively in the bowlers' favour. For example, Mynn's batting was good enough for him to be reckoned a leading all-rounder, even though in his twenty-five years of first-class cricket he made only one century. On the other hand, his career bowling figures – at least those that survive – credit him with 1,036 wickets at just over 10 runs each, an average that is twice as good as what would be very respectable 150 years later. Born in the village of Twisden in Kent, Mynn played his first-class cricket between 1834 and 1859, mostly for Kent, but also for, among others, Sussex and MCC. Mynn's unmistakable shape – drawings of him show the ample backside that is sometimes given as the main physical requirement for successful fast bowling – and explosive performances gained him wide recognition. In the summer of 1836, his health became a matter of national concern when he exacerbated a festering shin injury while making his one century for South v. North. Part of the problem was that it was considered unmanly, and unfair to bowlers, to wear 'leggings', as pads were then known. The *Leicester Journal* reported that he was 'obliged to be packed up, as it were, and laid on the roof of the stage coach, and in that position he rode from Leicester to London'. From a tavern in St Martin's Lane he was taken to St Bartholomew's Hospital, where, the rumour spread, his leg would be amputated. In fact it was saved and in time Mynn returned to his best. At a conservative estimate, he took 10 wickets in a match 34 times. When he died aged fifty-four, William Prowse wrote a poem in his memory that would take its place in the anthology of the best literature that cricket has inspired. It ended: 'Proudly, sadly will we name him – to forget him were a sin. / Lightly lie the turf upon thee, kind and manly Alfred Mynn!'

OLD TOM AND YOUNG TOM MORRIS
1821–1908 AND 1851–1875

TWO BEWHISKERED Tom Morrises played highly significant roles in developing golf in the nineteenth century. Old Tom, one of the game's first professionals, prepared the way for his son Young Tom, a tragic champion who came as close to being a sporting superstar as was possible at the time. The earliest professionals, while bearing little resemblance to modern tour players, were the forerunners of club pros in that they earned money from tuition. They also played for bets, caddied for the gentry and made equipment. Allan Robertson from St Andrews, who was born in 1815, is generally regarded as the first professional and Old Tom worked in his shop before the pair fell out over a new ball that Robertson tried to suppress because it was cheaper. The Morrises then set up their own manufacturing business in competition with Robertson. It was as players, though, that they became widely known, particularly through the Open championship that started in 1860 at the Prestwick Club. Despite the tournament's name, only professionals took part that year – amateurs made it truly open when they entered in 1861 – and Old Tom finished second, out of eight, in the inaugural event behind Willie Park Senior. Old Tom would win four of the next seven Opens before his son reeled off four in a row. Young Tom revolutionised the game with the help of the new iron clubs that replaced the wooden shafted ones (although his were a rather crude variety made by blacksmiths before new forging techniques brought the mass production of a more manageable kind). He progressed irons from being weapons with which to escape difficult lies, to instruments for driving, lofting and putting. Young Tom's first three Open victories were in successive years, 1868–70, which, the rules stipulated, meant he kept the silver-clasped, Moroccan-leather championship belt. It was partly through having to replace the trophy and partly to reappraise the championship in light of Young Tom's domination that the event did not take place in 1871. To reward clubs who contributed to the whip-round for the new trophy it was decided to rotate the venue, rather than always play at Prestwick. None of this affected Young Tom, who took the title again in 1872 to be the first winner of the elegant Claret Jug. Young Tom is the youngest player to have taken part in the Open, having been fourteen when he played in 1865 – a record that is unlikely to be beaten – and the youngest winner, at seventeen in 1868. He marked this first victory with a record low score of 154 for three rounds – the fourth round was added in 1892 – of the 3,799-yard course. It included the championship's first hole in one, at the 145-yard eighth hole. It was said of Young Tom Morris that he knew his worth and demanded and obtained a good living for the flair that he brought to the game. In this sense, he was the first true modern professional golfer. When Young Tom died at the age of twenty-four, soon after he lost his wife and child during childbirth, a broken heart was said to be the cause. 'If that was true I wouldn't be here either,' said Old Tom, who lived to be eighty-seven. A memorial at Young Tom's grave was inscribed:

'Deeply regretted by numerous friends and all golfers, he thrice in succession won the Championship Belt and held it without envy, his many amiable qualities being no less acknowledged than his golfing achievements.'

ARTHUR KINNAIRD
1847–1923

ARTHUR KINNAIRD, the 11th Lord Kinnaird, might have been remembered only as a nutty aristocrat, which he undoubtedly was, if he had not made such a stalwart contribution to football's emergence into the arc lights of popular entertainment. His main claim to recognition was as an administrator, but he had also been an extraordinarily energetic player whose presence was made more vivid by an unruly red beard and a fierce delight in aiming legal hacks at opponents' shins. In turn, he responded to hacks aimed at him 'without a trace of resentment'. A friend once reacted to Lady Kinnaird's concern that her husband would come home one day with a broken leg by saying: 'If he does, madam, it will not be his own.' The *Athletic News* praised him for being 'an exemplar of manly robust football', which helped to popularise the game 'among every class'. Kinnaird took part in nine FA Cup finals, including the second ever played in 1873. He was on the winning side five times, three of them with the Wanderers and two with the Old Etonians. In the days before more elaborate celebratory stunts, he marked the fifth of these successes, a 1–0 win by the OEs over Blackburn Rovers, by standing on his head in front of the pavilion at the Oval. Also in 1873, Kinnaird, whose family were from Perth, made his one appearance for Scotland in only the second ever officially recognised international, against England. He demonstrated his passion for football by playing in every position. As a goalkeeper and an outfield player, he scored goals for the Wanderers in successive FA Cup finals. In the 1877 2–1 win over Oxford University, playing as goalkeeper, he was credited with the first own goal in an important match after he stepped over his line having gathered an innocuous shot. The fact that it was not recorded as a goal at the time, the result for years being listed as 2–0, has led to speculation that it was the only instance of a player pulling aristocratic rank to manipulate a football scoreline. In 1878, after netting from half-back in a 3–1 win over the Royal Engineers, he was happier to have his goal appear in print. What is beyond question is his lordship's dynamic contribution as an administrator, his duties in this regard overlapping his playing days. He was a Football Association committeeman by the age of twenty-two and also served as treasurer. From 1890 to his death, he was the FA president. As a muscular Christian, he became Lord High Commissioner of the Church of Scotland.

BEST OF BRITISH

W. G. GRACE

PART THREE

AGE OF GRACE
1848–1899

W. G. GRACE
1848–1915

W. G. GRACE is probably the only nineteenth-century sportsman whose name remains familiar to a large number of
people. He enjoyed phenomenal success over more than forty
years, but his enduring fame is as much the triumph of an
extraordinary character as a great cricketer, given that he
excelled before it was fully formed as a national institution and
while sports reporting was still relatively restrained. He was
liable to be mobbed when he stepped off a train at Paddington
and was reckoned to be the second best-known Englishman of
his time after the politician William Gladstone. When William
Gilbert Grace was born in Downend, near Bristol, he joined
the growing brood of Dr Henry and Martha Grace.
Eventually they numbered nine children, all of them encouraged to play cricket, including the four girls. Grace was not
just a good cricketer. Aged eighteen, having scored 224 not out
at the Oval for 'England' against Surrey, he was given time off
to run in a hurdles race at Crystal Palace, which he won. He
was also a keen and competent bowls player. Grace was a
striking figure with his thickset trunk, which grew ever thick-
er given an appetite for food that matched his hunger for runs,
mighty forearms and prolific beard. But he was a mere
stripling when he first appeared in a representative match,
turning out aged nine for West Gloucestershire against
Bedminster. He matured quickly and through his mastery he
can now be seen as the founding father of the modern game.
His greatest contribution was as a batsman who broadened
the possibilities of strokeplay in defiance of traditions, such as
reserving front-foot shots for defence only, and poor batting

surfaces. 'There is one great landmark that separates the old batting from the new – the appearance of Dr W. G. Grace in the cricket world,' wrote K. S. Ranjitsinhji, himself an outstanding batsman. Grace played the first-class game, for Gloucestershire, London County and England, for forty-three years and at various times held nearly every batting record. He was the first to score double and triple hundreds, the first to make 2,000 runs in a season and the first to score one hundred centuries. His slow-to-medium bowling would have gained greater recognition had he not been such a fine batsman and fielded magnificently, particularly in the deep from where he propelled massive throws. At the Oval in 1878, a throw of his was officially recorded at 116 yards (106.07 metres). Grace played his cricket with a highly developed sense of his own importance; he was not above blatant cheating if he felt his continued presence on the field was desirable. Some matches had, after all, advertised: 'Admission threepence. If W. G. Grace plays admission sixpence'. He found time to qualify as a medical doctor, although, because of the distractions of cricket, it took him ten years. He coped with his two occupations as only a champion could, once spending all night at a patient's bedside before going out to score a double hundred.

MATTHEW WEBB
1848–1883

MATTHEW WEBB, generally known as Captain Webb, made his living – and his dying – from swimming. For the last eight years of his life, he undertook all manner of aquatic challenges. The most renowned of these, to become the first person to swim the English Channel, was gloriously realised, to the extent that newspapers called him 'probably the best known and most popular man in the world'. Stories of his prowess in the water marked his early life. He saved a brother from drowning in the Severn and, after joining the merchant navy, rescued a colleague while serving on a training ship in the Mersey. At twenty-six, he was awarded the first Stanhope gold medal by the Royal Humane Society, for an attempt to reach a seaman who had fallen overboard from a steamship. A year later, he resigned as a master mariner to prepare for his Channel swim. After an unsuccessful attempt to reach France, he set out a second time on 24 August 1875. His skin daubed with porpoise oil, he left from close to Admiralty Pier in Dover and was in the water for 21 hours 45 minutes. He was inspired as he approached the French coast by a mailship striking up 'Rule Britannia'. 'I felt a gulping sensation in my throat . . . [and] felt now I should do it,' he said. It was forty-eight years before anyone emulated him and eleven more after that before his time was beaten. Huge crowds welcomed him back to Shropshire, lining the route from Wellington station to Dawley, his birthplace. In London, the stock exchange raised £2,424 for a testimonial fund. Still, with a wife and two children, he had to keep devising ways to make his water pursuits profitable. He gave performances of swimming and diving at the Royal Aquarium in London and went to the US to cash in on the considerable impact he had made there. He won £1,000 for floating in a tank at the Boston horticultural show for 128 hours and collected substantial sums from prize races, including one off Nantasket beach in which he beat the US champion Paul Boyton. All this took its toll and a friend, who went to Niagara Falls to watch Webb's final stunt, compared this once handsome sailor 'with the broken-spirited and terribly altered appearance of the man who now courted death'. He stood to win £12,000 for swimming the rapids and whirlpools below the falls. He kept the attempt a secret from his wife, but thousands came to witness it. All went well until, according to one report, he 'abruptly threw up his arms and was drawn under'. His body was recovered four days later.

FRED ARCHER
1857–1886

FRED ARCHER killed himself at the age of twenty-nine, by which time he had comfortably exceeded what most jockeys would have been proud to achieve in a full life. With his distinctive style of sitting back 'and as it were driving his horse before him', he rode winners at a barely credible rate, as many as two per five rides at the height of his career. By his death he had raced on the flat for sixteen years, ridden 2,748 winners, twenty-one of them in English classics, including five Derbys, and been champion jockey from 1874 to 1886. Born in Prestbury, Gloucestershire, Archer was apprenticed to the trainer Matthew Dawson in 1870 and had his first winning ride the same year. His reputation for coaxing wins out of good and indifferent horses quickly spread and soon owners and trainers were turning to him before anyone else. Critics have sought to discredit him on the grounds that he was unduly severe on his mounts. One contemporary observer wrote: 'What might happen to a horse afterwards appeared to be no concern of his; his mind was set on winning the race he was at the moment contesting, and not a few two-year-olds on whom he had won were good for very little afterwards, his whip and spur having taken all the heart out of them.' The same writer also noted, though, that he was just as ready to be kind, once patting a horse on the neck midway through a five-furlong race to assure him that 'even at that early point of the struggle he had nothing to fear from any of his opponents'. Several theories for the reason, or reasons, behind his suicide have been suggested. They include depression, the pressure of maintaining his supremacy, the difficulty of keeping his weight down to around 8 stone 6 pounds (not easy for some-one who was 5 feet 10 inches with a natural weight of 11 stone), the death of his first child and then of his wife dur-ing the birth of their second child. It has been reported that when he shot himself he was in a state of delirium after drink-ing a disgusting concoction known as Archer's mixture, a purgative that was part of his weight-reducing regime. The sermon at his funeral contained this passage: 'And so the worn and wistful face, often such a true index of the secret streams of life within, seemed to speak of an undermining of the vital forces within; yea, was there not crammed into those sixteen years of an unparalleled career a spending of physical force which left nothing remaining but the framework of a used-up life.'

HARRY VARDON
1870–1937

HARRY VARDON went from reluctant golfer to winner of a record six Open championships and one US Open. As a child in Grouville, Jersey, he played only occasionally, despite having a course close to his home, and had no interest in being taught. When he started work as an apprentice gardener at the age of thirteen he seemed set for a very different outdoor life from the one that would gain him wide recognition. Older brother Tom, who would finish second to Harry in the 1903 Open, alerted Vardon to what professional golf might have to offer. Harry decided to take the game seriously himself and the combination of his affinity with it and the advantages of having a light frame, big hands and a placid temperament meant he moved quickly through the game's ranks. He would leave his name on countless trophies and on the overlapping grip that 'induces each hand to do its work properly' and still bears his moniker a century later. It was said of him, too, that he brought style to the swing and new standards of accuracy in a golden age of British golf that he shared with James Braid and John (JH) Taylor. The trio, born thirteen months apart, dominated the game in the twenty years before the First World War. They are also remembered for having imbued golf with an ethos of proper conduct that long outlived them. Vardon won his first Open in 1896, closing a six-stroke gap on Taylor on the last day before coming out on top in a 36-hole decider. He collected his sixth Open, at the age of forty-four, eighteen years later when his upright stance and flowing swing were still as impressive as they had ever been. 'Golfers find it a very trying matter to turn at the waist,' he said, 'more particularly if they have a lot of waist to turn.' When he won the US Open in 1900, by two shots, from Taylor, it was the first time the title had gone abroad. The winning margin would have been greater but for a 'whiff' on the final green when an uncharacteristically careless prod meant he missed the ball and a very short putt. He lost to the American amateur Francis Ouimet in a three-way playoff for the 1913 US Open title. Apart from his championship titles, Vardon had one other notable victory: in 1905 he and Taylor beat the Scottish pair Braid and Sandy Herd in a 72-hole challenge match for the considerable side-stake of £400.

LOTTIE DOD

1871–1960

LOTTIE DOD discarded tennis after winning Wimbledon five times in five attempts – she only ever lost five official matches in her entire career – to pursue the challenge of other sports. She was a champion golfer, hockey international, fine skater, the first woman to go down the Cresta Run and an Olympic medallist at archery. Had she been in Balaclava at the time, she would have no doubt led the Charge of the Light Brigade. The *Guinness Book of Records* named her and the American Babe Zaharias as the most versatile female athletes there had been. The daughter of wealthy parents from

Bebington, Cheshire, she started playing competitive tennis at eleven and by thirteen, having won her first titles, was dubbed Little Wonder by the press. At Wimbledon in 1887, she won the final 6–2 6–0 against Blanche Bingley, who, as defending champion, played only in the challenge match to decide the title. She was, at fifteen years 285 days, the youngest champion in the tournament's then brief history and, with no one younger having won the title more than a century later, she seems likely to retain the distinction in perpetuity. (In the 1990s an age restriction was imposed to stop burn-out.) Dod would beat Bingley, now known by her married name Blanche Hillyard, in each of her other finals in 1888, 1891, 1892 and 1893. She was credited with being the first woman to serve and volley and her feisty approach was reflected in an essay she wrote in 1897: 'For ladies, too, it is a very athletic exercise, always supposing that they go in for it heartily, and do not merely frivol at garden parties.' In August 1888, Dod, tired of the monotony of beating female opposition, played in the first 'battle of the sexes' against Ernest Renshaw in a match between the reigning Wimbledon champions. She lost but was reported to have made Renshaw 'run about as much as against a first-rate player of his own sex'. Dod's hockey career was brief but distinguished, her two goals against Ireland in 1900 securing a 2–1 win. Golf then took hockey's place and in 1904 she won the British ladies' championship at Troon by beating the favourite, May Hezlet. Dod and her brothers Willy and Tony were all keen archers. They may have felt they were upholding a family tradition, an ancestor having commanded the longbowmen at Agincourt. At the archery in the 1908 Olympics in London, Dod finished second behind Queenie Newall of Britain. She died aged eighty-eight during Wimbledon while listening to a broadcast of the championships from her nursing home bed.

C. B. FRY
1872–1956

C. B. (CHARLES BURGESS) FRY earned such a reputation for all-round sporting excellence that when in later life he remarked to a friend he might go in to horse racing, the friend asked: 'What as, Charles – trainer, jockey or horse?' Born in Croydon, Fry won a scholarship to Wadham College Oxford where he took a first in Classical Moderations and was a colossus of the games field. Wadham was said to consist of 'Fry and small fry'. His Blues included cricket and football and, but for injury, he would have gained another at rugby union. He gave up athletics after leaving Oxford having equalled the world long jump record of 23 feet 5 inches without the benefit of coaching or prolonged practice. He did not, though, abandon his party trick of doing a standing jump from the floor on to a mantelpiece. He continued to play cricket, the sport that most engaged him, and football, winning a cap for England against Ireland in 1901 and appearing at left back for Southampton in the 1902 FA Cup final. His first-class cricket career lasted thirty years, over which time he maintained a batting average of more than 50. He hit 94 hundreds, 6 of them in successive innings in 1901, which no one else managed until Donald Bradman nearly forty years later, but his bowling never recovered from the indignity of being called for throwing three times in 1898. James Phillips, the umpire who called him on the second occasion, compounded the hurt when he mockingly referred to him as

33

BEST OF BRITISH

C. B. FRY

'C. B. Shy'. He captained England in six of his twenty-six Tests, none of which was lost. His highest Test score of 144 at the Oval in 1905 demonstrated his versatility as a batsman. Australia set fields to block what they regarded as his strength, scoring in front of the wicket, which merely stimulated Fry's intellectual interest. He took it as a cue to remind himself how to cut, which by the end of his innings he was doing breathtakingly well. At Sussex, his batting with K. S. Ranjitsinhji illuminated the county scene, Fry's sinewy, pragmatic shot-making contrasting with his great friend's artistry. Fry's life beyond sport was full and varied. He and his wife spent forty years directing youth programmes on the training ship *Mercury*, which prepared boys for service in the Royal Navy. An association with the League of Nations spread his reputation further afield. 'It is quite on the cards that I might have been King of Albania,' he said after the Albanians sent a delegation to look for an English gentleman with £10,000 a year to sit on their throne. Fry qualified on the first count but not the second after he resisted pressing Ranji for a loan. He suffered recurring mental problems, while positive remarks about Nazism cast a shadow over an unusual life.

SYDNEY BARNES
1873–1967

SYDNEY BARNES arrived on the international scene with hardly a toot of a fanfare. 'Sydney Francis Barnes, a virtually unknown bowler selected by MacLaren, immediately demonstrated his artistry,' was how *Wisden* concealed its surprise after Barnes took seven wickets on his Test debut in Sydney in December 1901. Archie MacLaren, the England captain, had been entrusted with selecting the 1901–2 team to tour Australia and plucked the twenty-eight-year-old Barnes from the Lancashire League. MacLaren came across the bowler during a session in the nets: 'He thumped me on the left thigh. He hit my gloves from a length. He actually said, "Sorry, sir!" and I said, "Don't be sorry, Barnes. You're coming to Australia with me."' Barnes's apology suggests deference; on the contrary, he was a spiky individual who played for England until he was forty, but appeared in a mere 27 Tests – and still took 189 wickets at 16.43 each. Barnes knew about bolshiness long before it became de rigueur among top sportsmen. The writer Neville Cardus reckoned he was Mephistophelian in outlook, playing cricket not out of green field, starry-eyed idealism but because of the cash value of his talents. Even the admiring MacLaren found him hard to cope with, muttering on a rough sea crossing to New Zealand that the only consolation if they sank would be that 'that bugger Barnes will go down with us'. On the 1913–14 tour of South Africa, he refused to play in the final Test because a reward he claimed the host nation had promised him for agreeing to tour had not been forthcoming. He had taken 49 wickets at 10.93 in the first four Tests of that series – admittedly the matting pitches suited his

35

bowling – but he could not be persuaded to add to figures that more than ninety years later remained unmatched. He never played for England again. Barnes, born in Smethwick, played many more minor-county and league games than he did first-class matches. The daily toil of the county game did not particularly interest him and his appearances for Warwickshire, Lancashire and England amounted to just 133. He began, as young men tend to, as a fast bowler, but by the time MacLaren chose him he was a medium-paced spinner. He could swing and spin the ball in the space of the same delivery, turning it away from the direction it had swung. The ball with which he bowled Victor Trumper in the 1908 Adelaide Test started as an outswinger, turned from the off and hit Trumper's leg stump. Charlie Macartney, batting with Trumper, said it was 'the sort of ball a man might see if he was dreaming or drunk'. Barnes continued playing for Staffordshire into late middle-age. In his fifty-sixth year, he took 76 wickets for the county at 8.21 each.

GILBERT JESSOP
1874–1955

GILBERT JESSOP made a science of big hitting at a time when unreliable pitches meant even to swing discriminately at a cricket ball could be perilous. On the basis of one innings alone he was a champion of the game. At the Oval in the 1902 Test against Australia, England, needing 243 to win on a cart track, had subsided to 48 for 5 when Jessop joined F. S. Jackson. Extreme caution seemed the appropriate response. Jessop reached 50 in 43 minutes and was seventh out for 104 out of 139 made in 75 minutes. Soon afterwards, England got home by one wicket. No one, said C. B. Fry, drove a ball so hard, so high and in so many different directions. He cut devastatingly, too, and was an innovative and deadly leg-side hitter, which meant bowlers never quite knew what length or line to bowl at him. Born in Cheltenham, Jessop might have shone at a number of sports had he pursued them as eagerly as he did cricket. At Cambridge, he was close to representative standard at hockey and football, ran the 100 yards in 10.2 seconds and would have played billiards against Oxford had he not been gated because of his poor chapel attendance, particularly sinful for someone being groomed for the church. He was good enough at rugby union to appear as a three-quarter for Gloucester and as a scratch golfer he took part in the 1914 Amateur Championship. Of all these possibilities, cricket, batting, in particular, with its physical and mental challenges, most captivated him. 'Nerves play as important a part in batsmanship as skill,' he said lest anyone should mistake his innings for mindless romps. Jessop's calculated approach to the hazardous art of hitting out on suspect surfaces was reflected in his carefully worked-out stance. It earned him the nickname, which he disliked, of The Croucher. Only 5 feet 7 inches, he would bend low, the position from which he found it easiest to move in to a stroke, pounce forward or play the sweep, which he executed almost lying on the ground. The many startling statistics attached to his name include a scoring rate of just short of 100 runs an hour during the course of his five double-hundreds. He was so athletic it was said he could prevent singles standing 15 yards further back than any other cover fielder. A back injury meant he never fulfilled his early promise as a fast bowler. Although he did not play after the First World War for health reasons, he lived into his eighties.

JACK HOBBS
1882–1963

JACK HOBBS was too kind a man to want to embarrass anyone. Unavoidably, though, he made fools of the Essex committee members who rejected him. Hobbs, the most instinctive of batsmen, applied the discomfort as soon as he entered the first-class game, scoring 155 against Essex in his first championship match for Surrey in 1905, and rubbed it in over many years. The most remarkable Hobbs statistic was that he scored his hundredth hundred when he was forty and added 97 more before he retired aged fifty-one in 1934. Through 'those well-wrought centuries', wrote John Arlott in a poem about 'The Master', Hobbs 'reshaped the history of bat and ball'. Two things stopped him scoring even more runs: the First World War and his custom of sacrificing his wicket, once his team were strongly placed, so others could bat. He was widely seen as an even greater batsman than Donald Bradman in his ability to score heavily and unfussily no matter how tricky the surface. 'Hobbs is number one every time. He is so good on bad pitches,' said the England captain Douglas Jardine, who looked away, stonily, when asked if the competition included Bradman. Hobbs, the oldest of twelve children, was raised in Cambridge, where his father was groundsman and umpire at Jesus College. As a boy, he learnt to bat playing with college servants. They used a tennis ball and a stump for a bat and played on gravel, which may have accounted for his equable mood whatever the state of the pitch. One of the few sour notes in his career came on his first tour of Australia in 1907–8. He expected to make his Test debut in Sydney when a player fell ill on the eve of the match. Instead, George Gunn, who was not selected for the tour but was in Australia for health reasons, was picked. Hobbs felt badly treated and two weeks later in Melbourne, in the first of his 102 Test innings, injected a hint of 'I'll show you' as he made 83 in 195 minutes. His international career lasted until 1930; the previous year, aged forty-six, he had become Test cricket's most ancient century maker with 142 in Melbourne. Despite this, he said: 'I was never half the player after the First War than I was before.' There was a marked change

BEST OF BRITISH

JACK HOBBS

from supple strokemaker to a more prosaic style. Asked why those centuries he scored latterly were less dashing, he said: 'They were nearly all made off the back foot.' Still, he continued to prevail over bowlers of all types, maintaining Test and first-class averages of more than 50. He did it so unassumingly that even that least forgiving of cricketers, the scored-against fast bowler, bore him no grudge. 'It were 'ard work bowlin' at 'im,' said one, 'but it were something you wouldn't 'ave missed for nothin'.' He was knighted in 1953.

DOUGLAS CLARK
1891–1951

EVEN THE NORTH of England, proud of its many monuments to manliness, has produced few to compare with Douglas 'Duggy' Clark. Severely wounded at Passchendaele in the First

World War, Clark came home to a sporting career that had already been distinguished by enormous strength and fortitude. In 1914, in a rugby league Test match in Australia, Clark twice returned to the field after breaking bones to help a depleted England to an improbable victory. As a fearless wrestler, he won his first title at fifteen and continued in the sport for more than forty years. He was Army champion and held a version of the world heavyweight title. In one bout against Carver Doone, a 6 feet 8 inch Devonian who weighed more than 23 stones, he won by a knock-out despite conceding 100 pounds. Clark, who was born in Ellenborough in Cumberland, was eighteen when he signed to play rugby league for Huddersfield. He made the first team before completing a full season, even though his father asked that he should be kept back until he had matured physically. He went on to play 485 games for the club. Described as 'a giant on the football field in an age of giants', he was known for using his great bulk to maximum effect, but never unfairly. In 1915, he was a key member of the Huddersfield 'team of all talents' who won all four domestic competitions. He played in eight Tests against Australia and three against New Zealand and won seven caps for England in other internationals. The 1914 match against Australia in Sydney is remembered as the 'Rorke's Drift Test'. England secured the Ashes 2–1 with a 14–6 win, despite finishing with only ten men. Clark broke his thumb, pausing only briefly on the touchline while it was tightly bandaged. At the start of the second half, he went to hand off an Australia defender before remembering his broken thumb and opted instead to use his shoulder. As a result, he smashed his collar bone. Shoulder strapped, Clark made two attempts to rejoin his team-mates, who were slowly being depleted by other injuries, but finally had to accept that the pain was too great. He was wounded in eighteen places by shrapnel from a bomb during the war. He was also gassed twice and left blind for nine days. Doctors advised him to avoid strenuous exercise when he was discharged. Within two years he was playing Test rugby again.

MAX WOOSNAM
1892–1965

MAX WOOSNAM was a sportsman of storybook versatility who avoided the celebrity he never craved by living mostly in the first half of the twentieth century. Had it been the second half, when idolatry became fashionable, he would have found that his giddying round of achievements would have overwhelmed his inclination to avoid public acknowledgement. He captained Manchester City and England at football, at tennis he won a Wimbledon title and an Olympic gold medal and led the Davis Cup team, he scored a century at Lord's, played golf off scratch and made a 147 maximum break at snooker. He had a sporting pedigree of sorts. To solve the problem of living on the opposite bank of the Tyne from his future wife, Woosnam's father regularly swam across the river to meet her. His mother was a keen tennis player who was ahead of her time in playing a backhand when it was considered too vulgar a shot for a lady. His father Charles Woosnam was a priest; it was his wife Mary's money that enabled them to send their son Max to Winchester College and Cambridge. In 1911, while still at Winchester, Woosnam pulled off the first of his notable achievements, a century at Lord's for the public schools against MCC. At Cambridge, he won Blues in football, golf, tennis and real tennis. He shone at most games and dazzled at football and tennis, which was his preferred summer sport and explained why he played only two first-class cricket matches for the university. Woosnam's footballing talent was such that, while still at Cambridge, he played for Chelsea in a winter vacation, his three appearances all ending in wins without a goal being conceded. One report noted that Woosnam, who played at half back, 'in no way suffered by comparison with the best of his professional confrères'. Having survived the war, during which he saw action at Gallipoli and in the trenches in northern France, he went to work in Manchester where he was sought by both the town's great football teams. He signed for City in 1919 because United played some matches on Wednesday afternoons, when he would not have been available. Woosnam played 96 matches for City over four years. When he missed a match because of his job, workmates threatened to strike if it happened again. He was so popular with his professional team-mates that they voted him captain. In the summers he went off to play tennis with pyrotechnic enthusiasm. At the 1920 Olympics in Antwerp he won a gold medal in the doubles and a silver in the mixed doubles on the same day. In 1921, he won the Wimbledon doubles and was named captain of Britain's Davis Cup team to go to the US. He was also picked as captain of the national football team against Wales in 1922, a match England won 1–0, but suffered a broken leg the following year that led to his retirement from sport. In later life, Woosnam played social tennis.

JACK BERESFORD
1899–1977

JACK BERESFORD suffered a war wound that cost rugby union an outstanding prospect but gained Britain an oarsman whose many coups included infuriating the Führer. Unlike Steve Redgrave, who would also gather medals at five Olympics later in the century, Beresford mastered rowing and sculling to win golds in both the single and two-oared disciplines. Beresford, who was of Polish descent, chose rowing after he was badly wounded in the leg in France in the First World War. His rehabilitation, which included dinghy rowing off the Cornish coast, had reminded him how much he liked the sport. Beresford, who worked in the family furniture business, was small for an oarsman but was formidably strong in the upper body and thrived on hard training. At the age of twenty-one, he won a silver medal in the single sculls at the 1920 Olympics in Antwerp, losing to the American Jack Kelly by a second. Kelly was a bricklayer from Philadelphia, although he would later be better known as the father of Grace Kelly, who became Princess Grace of Monaco. Kelly had been banned from Henley that year because of his alleged professionalism, which was anathema to officials of the Royal regatta, and he may have viewed his hard-fought win over Beresford as a measure of revenge, although the two men grew to be firm friends. A story circulated that they were too exhausted to shake hands after the Antwerp race, which makes Kelly's victory in the double sculls half an hour later an heroic feat of recovery. In 1924 in Paris, Beresford easily won the single sculls, thanks to the introduction of the repêchage system. This meant that despite losing to the American William

43

Gilmore in the heats he was still able to reach the final. There he reversed the earlier result. Writing about the race, Gilmore recalled that the pain of losing was ameliorated by the smell from a scent factory wafting across the Seine. It made him feel he was rowing 'as if in a flowing river of the perfume itself'. Beresford switched to the eight for the 1928 Olympics in Amsterdam, where the crew won a silver behind the USA; according to the *New York Times*, the Americans' cox gave 'one of the greatest performances of demonical howling ever heard on a terrestrial planet'. At his last two Olympics Beresford won golds, in the coxless fours in 1932 in Los Angeles and the double sculls in 1936 in Berlin. Adolf Hitler, having seen Germany win five finals out five, watched crestfallen as Beresford, thirty-seven by now, and Dick Southwood struck back to break the German favourites in the double sculls in what Beresford called 'the sweetest race I ever rowed'. The indefatigable Beresford won the double sculls at Henley in 1939, but the war years that followed ended his hopes of going for a sixth Olympic medal.

FRANCIS CHICHESTER

PART FOUR

NEW CENTURIONS
1901–1916

FRANCIS CHICHESTER
⟶ 1901–1972 ⟵

FRANCIS CHICHESTER was a fearless yachtsman who took part in single-handed races. Most of them were against other sailors; all of them were battles that, as he put it, intensified life. The most notable challenge against absent rivals was when he set out from Plymouth in 1966 to beat the times of the great Victorian clipper ships to Australia. Having done this, he paused for just over a month before setting sail again to complete a circumnavigation of the globe that broke numerous records. He was fêted in Britain, where he was knighted by Queen Elizabeth II. He also received this equivocal recognition from an American magazine: 'The gaunt, 65-year-old mariner, whose solo navigation of the globe ended last week, became the hottest commercial property in hero-starved Britain since Twiggy [the 1960s model].' Chichester, born in Barnstaple, Devon, was eighteen when he emigrated to New Zealand where he learnt to fly, a pastime that became the focus of his early adventures. On a visit to England in 1929, he took delivery of a de Havilland Gipsy Moth aircraft. Mechanical problems meant he failed to beat the record for a solo flight to Australia on his way back to New Zealand. An attempt to fly around the world on his own ended when he struck overhead cables and sustained serious injuries, but he did complete the first solo flight across the Tasman Sea from Auckland to Australia. During the Second World War, he wrote the navigation manual used by single-handed fighter pilots. In 1958, he was diagnosed with cancer and given six months to live. His wife refused to let surgeons operate and nursed him back to health. In 1960, Chichester entered the first single-handed transatlantic sailing race, which he co-founded and took part in 'to complete my cure'. He won the race in *Gipsy Moth III*, crossing from Plymouth to New York in 40 days, which shortened the record by 16 days. Chichester's 1966 voyage in *Gipsy Moth IV* from Plymouth to Sydney took 107 days, compared to the 123 days averaged by the nineteenth-century clippers. The maximum speed of a yacht is related to its wetted length and while *Gipsy Moth IV* was 53 feet, the clippers were more than 200 feet. Also, Chichester had to set in excess of 1,500 square feet of sail on his own. He had been at sea for 226 days when he sailed back into Plymouth in May 1967. He had, among other things, completed the first one-stop circumnavigation, more than doubled to 15,500 miles the longest passage by a small vessel without a port of call and set a record for single-handed speed by sailing 1,400 miles in eight days. In July 1967, the Queen knighted him at Greenwich using the sword that Queen Elizabeth I gave to Sir Francis Drake.

JOE DAVIS
1901–1978

JOE DAVIS turned what might have been a misspent youth into a decent living for himself and a crusade that would provide the British public with a new sporting entertainment. He was fixated on billiards as a child, but realised that the three-ball game would never gain mass appeal because of the extraordinary proficiency of the top players. 'Virtually alone in his assessment of snooker's potential, he persuaded the Billiards Association to sanction an inaugural world snooker championship in 1927,' wrote the snooker commentator and historian Clive Everton. Thus he propelled into the spotlight a nascent sport that in 1985 would attract a TV audience of 18.5 million to watch Dennis Taylor beat Steve Davis in the world final. Born in Whitwell, Derbyshire, Davis watched the clients at his father's hotel play billiards, taking it up himself when he was big enough. At twelve he made his first break of 100; at twenty-one he played in the world professional billiards championship; and between 1928 and 1932 he won the event on the four occasions it was held. Having championed snooker, Davis then became its unbeatable champion. He won the first world professional championship in 1927 to land a prize of £6.50 and retained the title up until 1946. His younger brother Fred made the fraternally loaded observation: 'Joe was a great player before anyone else knew how to play the game.' It was also the case, though, that through his devotion to snooker Davis developed it into a credible sport almost single-handed. As the success of the professional game grew, Davis exercised a godfatherly control, assessing commercial deals and decid- ing who should join the paid ranks. He stopped playing, in the world championships, after 1946 but continued to compete in other events and achieved the first officially recognised 147 break in 1955. Davis's fear of being humiliated in the sport he pioneered was the subject of much gossip. It was said to be the reason he stopped playing in the world championship and why, so he had an excuse for losing, he would give opponents a few blacks' start. Brother Fred was the only player to whom he lost on level terms. Davis's withdrawal from the world championship did have the effect of diminishing snooker's popularity, and it was not revived until television latched on to the sport's appeal. Davis died soon after collapsing while watching a world semi-final at the Crucible Theatre, Sheffield.

ERIC LIDDELL
1902–1945

WHEN THE TIME CAME to choose, Eric Liddell picked running from a number of sports at which he excelled. The Scotsman, who was born in China and whose missionary parents sent him to boarding school in England, was also outstanding at rugby and cricket. A devout Christian, he wore his athletic brilliance lightly. He was, said his headmaster, entirely without vanity. The 1981 film *Chariots of Fire*, based on the 1924 Paris Olympics, accurately portrayed Liddell as a singular man and athlete who ran in a peculiar way – with his head thrown back and mouth wide open. But it also used dramatic licence freely. Liddell's astonishing recovery to make up a 20-yard deficit after falling in an international 440-yard race took place in a match against England and Wales and not, as the film had it, in a needle contest between Scotland and France. The greater departure from the real script, though, was that the film had Liddell pulling out of the Olympic 100 metres, his preferred distance, at the last minute after learning late on that the heats were on a Sunday. In the film, a Lord Burleigh figure then stepped aside to offer him his place in the 400. In fact, Liddell knew the schedule some months beforehand and made it known that his Christian principles would not allow him to run on a Sunday. This left him plenty of time to prepare for the 200 and 400 metres, in which Lord Burleigh was not entered. Liddell was third in the 200 metres final on 9 July and the next day ran respectable times in the first two rounds of the 400 metres. On the morning of 11 July, he broke 49 seconds for the first time, but was slower than the winner of the other semi-final, the American Horatio Fitch. The final, later the same day, saw Liddell adopt the seemingly suicidal tactic of sprinting the first half of the race in 22.2 seconds, only 0.3 second slower than his bronze-medal time in the 200. Instead of fading, he actually extended his lead to win by more than five metres in an Olympic record 47.6 seconds. Liddell's triumph was marked by a parade through the streets of Edinburgh. He followed his parents into missionary work in China and in 1943, during the second Sino-Japanese war, was interned in a Japanese camp under a brutal regime. He died of a brain tumour while still incarcerated. In 1991, Edinburgh University marked his burial place at the camp with a stone of Mull granite; the Eric Liddell centre was set up in the old North Morningside Church in Edinburgh, where he was an active member during his student days.

WALTER HAMMOND
1903–1965

WALTER 'WALLY' HAMMOND stands as comfortably in the company of the greatest cricketers as he did at the crease when batting at his most majestic. At Lord's in 1938, Ernie McCormick, bowling the quickest of his quick spells in a short Test career for Australia, reduced England to 31 for 3 before Hammond took command. He consumed McCormick's fire in a conflagration of his own. As ever, unhurried, athletic foot movement and the assertive arc of powerful arms character- ised his batting in a six-hour innings of 240 whose only chance split a fieldsman's finger. It was perhaps the greatest of his 36 double-centuries, a figure surpassed only by Donald Bradman. Bradman rated the self-taught Hammond the strongest off- side player – off front foot and back – he ever saw; Alec Bedser, of Surrey and England, reckoned him the greatest all-rounder, testimony to the medium-fast, occasionally disconcertingly quick, bowling that lurked menacingly in the shadow of his batting. He was also a wonderful slip fielder. In private, Hammond could be moody and withdrawn; on the cricket field he was composed and engaged. On the few occasions he was ruffled it was because he disapproved of the spirit in which the game was being played. He once bowled an over of underarm grubs when Lancashire were scoring deliberately slowly. Hammond, whose father was killed in action in the First World War, was born in Kent. By 1918, the family had settled in Gloucestershire, the county with which Hammond started his thirty-one-year association in 1920. 'The possibilities of this boy Hammond are beyond the scope of estimation,' wrote Neville Cardus. His opportunities early on were restricted, partly because his qualifications for Gloucestershire was disputed as it was not his county of birth. Also, he con- tracted an illness in the West Indies which meant he did not play at all in 1926. Strong evidence emerged that this was a social disease that made a misery of his later life. In 1927, he scored 1,000 runs in May and played in his first Test in South Africa later that year. Despite the intervention of the Second World War towards the end of his career – he appeared in eight postwar Tests – Hammond played eighty-five times for

England, made 336 not out at faster than a run a minute against New Zealand in Auckland in 1933 and finished with a Test batting average of 58.45 after being top scorer with 79 in his last innings, also against New Zealand, when he was forty-three. He died in South Africa aged sixty-two never having fully recovered from a motor accident five years earlier.

HAROLD LARWOOD
1904–1995

HAROLD 'LOL' LARWOOD's fast bowling reverberated in the age in which he played and down the years that followed even though he appeared in only 21 Test matches. He was a central figure on the 1932–3 Ashes tour that featured cricket's bitterest Test series. Larwood and his polar opposite, Douglas Jardine, England's icily patrician captain, regarded the 'leg theory' as a legitimate means of securing victory; others saw it as no more than a cynical exercise in denying Donald Bradman runs through intimidation – and knew it as the 'Bodyline series'. Larwood answered all the romantic notions of an England fast bowler. He was born in the mining village of Nuncargate, left school at thirteen, worked as a pit-boy and never lost the habit of reaching for a beer and fag whenever a break in play permitted. A life in the mines gave way to one as a professional cricketer after he brought terror to village and junior league matches. At nineteen he signed for Nottinghamshire, where he built up his pace to be genuinely quick, able to discomfit all but those with the steadiest and steeliest of nerves. When he delivered his fastest ball, at the end of a rhythmical, 18-yard run-up, it was said his right hand began close to his calf and ended with its knuckles scraping the pitch. In 1925, aged twenty, he took 73 wickets in twenty matches and, picked by England the following summer, he played a significant role in winning the fifth Test and regaining the Ashes. Larwood did well on the 1928–9 tour of Australia, which saw the Ashes retained despite Bradman's ominously successful emergence on the Test scene. Bradman's triple-century, two double-centuries and plain old single-century in the 1930 Tests in England persuaded Jardine that something had to be done in 1932–3 – and in Larwood he found the perfect accomplice, priming him at clandestine meetings before the tour. The Adelaide Test was the most dramatic. Bill Woodfull was struck over the heart by Larwood, which prompted Jardine to apply more bodyline pressure when Australia's captain recovered. Larwood then hit Bert Oldfield, who suffered a fractured skull. Mounted police gathered as the spectators grew restless. The respective governments were even drawn in to the dispute over the fast bowler's line of attack. Larwood, who refused to sign a letter of apology, did not play again for England after this series, despite being hailed as a hero at home. Reviled for a while in Australia, Larwood returned to live happily there until he died at the age of ninety.

GORDON RICHARDS
1904–1986

GORDON RICHARDS, who had only ever sat on a pit pony before the age of fourteen, became one of the very finest of thoroughbred riders. 'I can't remember ever being told how to ride,' he said. 'I just got on a pony's back and away I went.' His father, a miner, reared the ponies that gave Richards his rudimentary introduction to the art of horsemanship. A number of trainers near the family home in Shropshire regarded the style Richards stuck to throughout his racing career – a long rein and upright stance – as more suited to a Skegness donkey and turned down his application for work. He eventually went to Jimmy White's stable in Wiltshire, where his winning goal in a football match against a neighbouring stable secured White's pay-out on a wager. Richards's reward was a ride the next day in which he confirmed the promise that his employer had begun to suspect. He won his first race at Leicester in 1921 when he was still only sixteen and in 1925, having served his apprenticeship, was champion jockey with 118 winners. He contracted tuberculosis, but emerged from his convalescence having made an important contact. Bill Rowell, a fellow patient in a Norfolk clinic, became a sort of Professor Higgins to his new-found friend, coaching Richards in the arcane ways of the high society in which he was about to mix. His 259 wins in 1932 broke a record that had stood for nearly fifty years and by now his name was synonymous with winning – even if the prize of a Derby victory still eluded him. This continued in 1942, when he won all the big races on King George VI's horses except the mile-and-a-half classic, and in 1947, when he won 269 other races. With dramatic timing, Richards kept the nation waiting until the week in 1953 when Queen Elizabeth II was crowned, Everest was conquered and Richards himself became Sir Gordon, the first jockey to be knighted. Pinza, at an imposing 16 hands, provided a suitable perch for a new knight riding in the Derby and the pair swept to victory. A huge crowd watched Pinza relegate the Queen's own horse, Aureole, into second place, which, at least, pleased the headline writers: 'Half a million groaned for Elizabeth the SECOND'. The victory helped Richards to his twenty-sixth jockeys championship. In 1954, he broke his pelvis and retired, having ridden 4,870 winners from 21,843 mounts. He stayed in racing for fifteen years as a trainer.

HENRY COTTON
1907–1987

HENRY COTTON had a predilection for toil and pleasure in almost equal measure. He even practised his golf between rounds, which was unheard of in the 1930s, hitting balls out of thick rough until his hands bled. In all probability, he would soothe away the pain with a bottle of champagne, the only possible accompaniment for caviar, having first changed from immaculate golf clothes into something equally well tailored for the clubhouse. He would then drive his Rolls-Royce to wherever he was living at that time: the five-star hotel at which for a while he had a suite, perhaps, or the estate he bought in later life. Cotton, who was born in Cheshire, spent what would almost certainly have been the best years of his golfing life serving in the Royal Air Force. That the Second World War deprived him of many titles is demonstrated by the spacing of his three Open championships: 1934, 1937 and 1948. His sporting vocation had seemed likely to be cricket, until he left school after falling out with the coach. He took up golf and turned professional at not quite seventeen, a particularly young age for a 1920s middle-class public schoolboy. His move would help to break down the social barrier that had existed between professionals and amateurs. He dominated the 1934 Open at Royal St George's, Sandwich, after a record first two rounds of 132 (67, 65). Dunlop named its 65 ball in honour of the second round, which consisted of only threes and fours. Even with a final round of 79, he won by five strokes. Barred from the clubhouse as a professional, he received the trophy dressed in an overcoat because he did not have time to retrieve a jacket from his car-cum-changing room. He clinched his second Open at Carnoustie with a round of 71, which, considering it took place in a rainstorm, was reckoned to be as impressive as the 65 at George's. He was forty-one by the time he won his third Open at Muirfield in 1948. His straight hitting – only four of his 56 drives missed fairways – prompted one rival to comment: 'You could not tell whether he was left or right he was so close to the middle.' King George VI, the only reigning monarch to attend a day at the championship, could not have chosen more perfectly. He was there to watch Cotton's course-record 66 that put him beyond the reach of his pursuers. Cotton, who played in four Ryder Cups, continued to make an impact on golf into old age as coach, author and course designer. He was, above all, a man of style – and aphorisms. 'The best is always good enough for me,' was one of a number of very good ones.

FRED PERRY
1909–1995

FRED PERRY turned a talent for striking a tennis ball into a passport to a life that could hardly have been further removed from its humble beginnings. His tennis career was dazzling enough. He won all the grand slam tournaments, including Wimbledon three years in a row from 1934 to 1936, and raised England to the forefront of the world game. His picaresque journey beyond tennis provided additional glister. It embraced marriages to four beautiful women, ownership of the Beverly Hills Tennis Club, with its celebrity-studded membership, and an eponymous clothing brand. Perry was born in Stockport, near Manchester, the son of parents who worked in the cotton industry. His father, Sam, had political ambitions – he would become a Labour MP – which led the family to move to the London suburb of Ealing. It was here during his schooldays that Perry's proficiency at ball games emerged. A self-taught table tennis player, he made rapid headway to gain selection for England. At the age of twenty he won the world title in Budapest, where a non-Hungarian had never triumphed in an international event. By now, he had already latched on to tennis and again he made swift progress, developing his table-tennis forehand into a whipped and destructive tennis stroke. Ambition, talent and dedication drove him in these early days; later a lust for competition and a keen eye for ways to gain an advantage made him a resolute and – to many opponents – annoying match player. His habit of saying 'Very clevah' when a rival hit a good shot had the irritating effect Perry intended. He won his first grand slam title in the US in 1933 but his most impressive triumph came the following year when he claimed the first of his three Wimbledon titles. Perry's working-class background meant neither the crowd nor Wimbledon officials, who were from a very different social milieu, were as effusive as they might have been. This was one reason Perry moved to the United States, where he took out citizenship. The Americans liked the tall, good-looking Englishman as much as he liked them, particularly their women. In Los Angeles, where he played regularly in the Pacific Southwest championships, he soon fell in with the film set. In 1935, he wed the Hollywood actress Helen Vinson, the first of three unsuccessful liaisons before a fourth and lasting marriage. Perry won eight grand slam titles and played the lead role in four Davis Cup wins, but was excluded from such events after turning professional in 1936. The true measure of what Perry achieved coming from a country apathetic towards competitive tennis – beyond putting on the annual Wimbledon show – was the chronic failure of British men either side of his many triumphs.

SYDNEY WOODERSON
1914–2006

SYDNEY WOODERSON was among the most respected of the what-might-have-been generation whose years of sporting maturity were spent serving their country in the Second

World War. Wooderson, born in London, won a place in the public's affections because, although he was not much bigger than a jockey at 5 feet 6 inches and under 9 stone, he could generate enough horsepower on his own to outrun much longer-striding rivals. He was also admired for his loyalty to the grass roots of his sport. He regarded his club, Blackheath Harriers, as his greatest responsibility and set his world records not in the big arenas, but at club meetings on suburban tracks. The most notable example was his world mile record of 4 minutes 6.4 seconds at Motspur Park in 1938. When he did submit himself to a big occasion at London's White City in August 1945, a crowd of 54,000 filled the stadium, while thousands more gatecrashed, including a certain Mr Bannister and his son Roger. The attraction was a mile race in which Wooderson took on the Swedes Arne Andersson and Gunder Hagg. Sweden's neutrality meant Andersson and Hagg had spent the war years trimming the world mile record. Wooderson, on the other hand, had had little chance to train seriously. Although his war service was restricted by poor eyesight, he had worked as a fireman during the Blitz and as an Army engineer. He had also been struck down by rheumatic fever and told he would never run again. He put this prognosis to flight with a gallant performance that saw him succumb to Andersson's superior fitness only in the finishing straight. In a rematch in Gothenburg, he held out almost until the tape only for Andersson to pass him again. He was thirty-one by now but his 4 minutes 4.2 seconds for the mile and a British record 3 minutes 48.4 seconds for the 1500 metres hinted at the times he might have recorded had he not been denied a running career in his late twenties. Wooderson might well have preceded Bannister to the first sub-four-minute mile – he set a world best of 2 minutes 59.5 seconds for three-quarters of a mile nearly two decades before Bannister's historic run – and would surely have won medals at the cancelled Olympics of 1940 and 1944. In 1937 he set world records for the 880 yards and 800 metres (1 minute 49.2 seconds and 1 minute 48.4 seconds) and with a fast run of 3 minutes 53.6 seconds won the 1938 European 1500 metres title. A year after the war, he was first in the European 5,000 metres in Oslo, but in winning the English cross-country title in 1948 he suffered a career-ending Achilles tendon injury. Soon afterwards at the Olympic Games in London, Gaston Reiff of Belgium won the 5,000 metres in a time 9 seconds slower than Wooderson had run in beating him in Oslo two years before. By then Wooderson was officiating at club meetings when his work as a solicitor allowed.

STANLEY MATTHEWS
1915–2000

STANLEY MATTHEWS had no idea how he wove together the strands of his genius. 'It just comes out of me under pressure,' was about the best he could manage. The fastidious care he took of himself – his light was always out by 9 p.m. – and his addiction to hard training obviously helped, but they merely nurtured what nature had given him: the body swerve, the uncanny ability to make the ball do his bidding and the explosive speed from a standing start. He was the original 'Wizard of the Dribble', the classic outside right who somehow persuaded left backs to move inside and allow him passage between them and the touchline. 'You usually knew

BEST OF BRITISH

STANLEY MATTHEWS

how he'd beat you, but you couldn't do anything about it,' said the Tottenham Hotspur captain Danny Blanchflower. Matthews's name on a team sheet was reckoned to add 10,000 to the gate. The son of a boxer, he caused excitement almost from the day he first kicked a football. He joined the Stoke City ground staff when he left school at fourteen, played in the reserve side in the Central League when he was fifteen and, after signing as a professional at seventeen, played his first full season on the right wing for the club in 1932–3. He went on playing until after his fiftieth birthday in 1965, the year he became football's first knight, by which time he had returned to Stoke for his final years. He had fallen out with them in 1947 – the Stoke manager, Bob McGrory, reckoned the thirty-two-year-old Matthews was past it – and joined Blackpool for £11,500. In all he appeared in 886 first-class matches, including 54 internationals for England (or 84 with wartime fixtures) between 1934 and 1957. At forty-two he was the country's oldest international. In 1956, aged forty-one, he reduced the world's best left back, Nilton Santos, to faltering ineptitude as he created three goals in England's 4–2 win over Brazil at Wembley. Another match, though, came to symbolise Matthews's light-footed artistry. In the 1953 FA Cup final, Stan Mortensen scored a hat-trick for Blackpool that was of secondary significance to the mayhem Matthews caused on the left of Bolton's defence to turn a 3–1 deficit into a 4–3 victory. That same year, Matthews had the chastening experience of playing in England's 6–3 defeat by Hungary at Wembley, a result that damaged British football's reputation while leaving Matthews's intact. The dedication on a statue of Matthews outside the Stoke City ground reads: 'His name is symbolic of the beauty of the game, his fame timeless and international, his sportsmanship and modesty universally acclaimed. A magical player, of the people, for the people.'

ALEXANDER OBOLENSKY
1916–1940

ALEXANDER OBOLENSKY became the emblem of a lost generation of gilded youth. He played rugby union four times for England and died soon after his twenty-fourth birthday. A fleeting passage of play in the first of his international appearances and his death, in the cockpit of a fighter plane in 1940, ensured his memory survived in perpetuity. If anything, the fact that he was a Russian prince enhanced his image as the symbol of a romantic age when games playing and dying young were things done stylishly by people with exotic names. Obolensky, born in St Petersburg, played his rugby with a panache appropriate to his image; his death, though, was more prosaic. Having joined the RAF's 54 Squadron, he broke his neck during training when his Hurricane Mark I dropped off the runway at Martlesham Heath, Suffolk. Obolensky's parents, Prince Serge – an officer in the Tsar's Imperial Horse Guards – and Princess Luba, fled Russia after the revolution of 1917 and settled in Muswell Hill, north London. Prince

Alexander, who would later drop his royal title, was educated at Trent College in Derbyshire before going to Oxford University where he played in two Varsity matches, his speed and hard tackling on the right wing being features of both his appearances. Obolensky's selection for his England debut in January 1936, when he was still only nineteen, caused a minor stir because he was not yet officially a British citizen. His subsequent performance against the third All Blacks could be construed as one of the more impressive applications for official residency. He travelled to the match with the England captain, B. C. Gadney, and the pair got off the train three stops before Twickenham to warm up by running the last two miles. Thus invigorated, Obolensky scored two tries in England's 13–0 victory, the first time they had beaten the All Blacks. In the twenty-eighth minute, Obolensky touched down for a try that was as straightforward as his second, ten minutes later, was spellbinding. He came infield when the movement carrying the ball towards him straightened, took a pass from fly-half Peter Chandler on an angled run, something that was not yet a standard manoeuvre, and, with his head back and fair hair flowing, maintained the line for 70 yards, scattering and dumbfounding the New Zealand defence as he sliced through to the opposite corner. Footage of the try, complete with pukka voiceover, became a Movietone News classic. Obolensky failed to score another try in his three other appearances for England.

STIRLING MOSS

PART FIVE

DASHING AND DARING
1918–1934

DENIS COMPTON
1918–1997

DENIS COMPTON was a charmed sportsman whose natural ability as a cricketer and footballer saved him from the consequences of chronic ineptitude in other areas, notably in the matter of organising himself. His success led to others bringing order to his life so that, after time and injury had done their worst, he could continue being a genial roué into old age. Aside from an unusual facility for playing games, Compton was born with few advantages. The family just about got by on his father's modest earnings as a decorator in north London and later a lorry driver. Compton scored heavily in schools cricket and made his debut for Middlesex in 1936 aged eighteen, batting at number 11. He made 14 and the umpire Bill Bestwick said he gave him out lbw only because he wanted a pee. In 1937 he scored 1,980 runs and played his first Test match against New Zealand. His adventurous, carefree strokeplay and pin-up good looks made him popular with a public depressed by the prospect of world war in the 1930s and demoralised afterwards by its lingering deprivations. He scored 3,816 runs in the summer of 1947, an aggregate that may never be surpassed. His career batting average stayed above 50 in 78 Tests and 515 first-class matches. Apart from his right-handed batting, Compton bowled left-arm spin sufficiently well to take 622 wickets and ran atrociously between the wickets. One team-mate reckoned that a call for a run from Compton was no more than a basis for negotiation. His football career also took off in 1936 when he made his debut on the left wing for Arsenal, scoring in a 2–2 draw with Derby County. He made wartime appearances for England, but his football feats never matched what he achieved

BEST OF BRITISH

DENIS COMPTON

in cricket. He said himself he was too selfish on the ball and progressive knee trouble held him back. Still, in 1950 he regained his Arsenal place during their FA Cup run and, with his brother Leslie, was in the XI who won the Wembley final 2–0 against Liverpool. Compton's disordered life beyond sport was illustrated by the suitcase full of unopened letters he presented to a reporter in 1949. Inside one was an offer of £2,000 to write a newspaper column; another was an indignant follow-up withdrawing the offer because of Compton's silence. As a result, Compton hooked up with Bagenal Harvey, the first sportsman's agent, who did the deal with Brylcreem that made Compton's hair the most famous in Britain. After he retired from cricket, he was an uncritical broadcaster and correspondent for a Sunday newspaper, a successful glad-hander for advertising agencies and a convivial companion at the bar. His memorial service at Westminster Abbey created a bigger demand for tickets than any in thirty years.

JIM LAKER
1922–1986

JIM LAKER had a wry view of life, his own included. 'The older I get, the better cricketer I seem to become,' he said long after his retirement. It was a typically droll reflection on how the golden glow of 'Laker's Match' spread gradually to shine on the whole of his career. He had a point. His 19 wickets for 90 in the 1956 Test at Old Trafford against Australia – figures unsurpassed in first-class cricket, let alone in Tests – were, inevitably, unrepresentative of nearly two decades of spin bowling. Laker knew, too, that a set of circumstances came together for him in that match: a poor batting side, who were unused to finger spin, caught on a grassless pitch that responded keenly to the torque his strong fingers put on the ball – and laws that still allowed 'a leg trap' of close fielders. With his Yorkshireman's sense of nowt was worth shouting about, he never let himself forget that his historic feat owed a certain amount to good fortune. Nor did he mind at all that on the way back from Old Trafford he sat in a pub eating a sandwich with no one noticing him, and he was amused that when he arrived home his wife, weary from answering the phone, asked: 'Jim, did you do something good today?' But if Laker himself liked to talk down his 19 wickets, those with no interest in perpetuating Northern modesty gave the performance the place it deserved in the canon of great cricketing achievements. The salient fact was he bowled in tandem at Old Trafford with Tony Lock, his Surrey team-mate and possibly the world's second-best slow bowler at the time – and all Lock could manage was the solitary dismissal that eluded Laker. Lock took the third wicket in Australia's first innings, after which Laker tidied up with 7 for 8 in 22 balls. Rain stopped Laker spinning England to victory before the fourth day, when he finished with second innings figures of 10 for 53 to go with his 9 for 37 in the first innings. Laker, born in Frizinghall, Bradford, joined Surrey after being billeted in London before leaving the Army. His 66 wickets in 1947 gained him elevation to the Test team. He never found it easy to command a place, but was always liable to return startling figures: 8 wickets for 2 runs in a Test trial in 1950 and all 10 again against the 1956 Australians, this time for Surrey. He was a key player for Surrey in their seven consecutive county championships in the 1950s. An autobiography, in which he criticised the England and Surrey captain Peter May, upset the authorities, but he remained popular with the public and established a new career as a TV commentator before he died aged sixty-four.

MICK THE MILLER
1926–1939

MICK THE MILLER was the brindled dog who lifted the spirits of thousands at a time of economic hardship. The 1920s and 1930s were probably the only years when greyhound racing could have prospered quite as spectacularly as it did. The blessing was that the time of opportunity and Mick the Miller coincided, answering a need for entertainment that was real, exciting, accessible, inexpensive and had a genuine star. Inner-city dog tracks became citadels of escapism that men and women, struggling to exist on meagre budgets, could reach at minimal cost. They were swept up by the thrill of the racing and the chance to make a small profit from a modest flutter. Mick the Miller was as brilliant and honest and cunning an athlete as any who talked rather than barked. When he was in town, the anticipation infiltrated every household in the community. He raced for only three years, 1929 to 1931, but his reputation soared so rapidly he drew crowds of up to 70,000. Ireland, the country of Mick's birth, did not have dog racing at

the time – in fact the sport barely existed in Britain. Mick's arrival on the scene – he was brought over to race at London's White City by a parish priest named Father Martin Brophy – helped to change all that. The central plot of Mick's story concerned three Greyhound Derbys, starting with 1929. In the first round of that 1929 race, Mick broke the half-minute barrier for the traditional Derby distance, 525 yards, to set a world record of 29.82 seconds. This prompted Father Brophy to cash in straightaway and accept a colossal £800 offer for his dog. In the final, which was rerun after a three-dog pile-up, Mick performed magnificently, skimming low and long to a three-length victory. When he won a second time in 1930, during a sequence of nineteen straight victories, the King of Spain was among the crowd of 50,000 who watched him dominate the final. The 1931 final was unbearably dramatic for the thousands who gathered at White City to witness Mick the Miller's third-in-a-row. A serious rival had emerged, Ryland R, a beast of a dog at 80 pounds who flew out of the traps while Mick struggled at the back. But Mick delivered one of his greatest races to surge through and beat Golden Hammer by a head. The hubbub turned from one of joyous celebration to rumbling menace when the red light signalling 'no race' shone out from the results board. 'My darling Mick has won,' sobbed his owner, Phiddy Kempton, but the decision to invalidate the result stood even though Mick had been blameless in the incident that led to the rerun. Mick slipped early in the second running, never showed and finished fourth behind Seldom Led. If anything the defeat enhanced the legend of Mick the Miller, who starred in the 1934 film *Wild Boy*. When he died, his stuffed and mounted body was displayed at the Natural History Museum.

FRED WINTER
1926–2004

FRED WINTER had such an immense talent as a jump jockey and trainer that it prevailed over his inclination to find some other way of making a living. Partly because of his rising weight, he failed to emulate the flat-racing success of his father, who had won the 1911 Oaks at the age of sixteen. He was not enthused by the prospect of switching to jump racing, an antipathy that deepened when he broke his back on his eleventh ride. He also said he would never become a trainer because, 'Frankly, I don't know enough about horses.' In one of the great triumphs of achievement over aversion, Winter went on to become the only person to win the Grand National, Champion Hurdle and Gold Cup as a trainer and jockey. Winter had his first public ride at Newbury when he was thirteen and weighed 5 stone 7 pounds. He finished ninth out of 21 although the horse, Tam O'Shanter, did provide him with his first winner soon afterwards at Salisbury. He went to Newmarket to join Henry Jellis as an apprentice, but, after managing only two wins in eighty rides, and with his weight problem increasing, he decided to convert to jump racing. On his second day he rode the first of his 923 winners, a record that included four champion jockey titles, two Grand National triumphs, two victories in the Gold Cup and three in the Champion Hurdle. As a trainer, he was champion eight times and repeated his successes in the National Hunt calendar's three biggest races. Winter's skill as a horseman became legendary after the 1962 French Grand National at Auteil in which he rode Mandarin, whose rubber bit broke at the fourth of 30 fences. Anyway, feeling unwell with stomach trouble, Winter was now left with no brakes or steering, nor was there any rail to help him keep Mandarin on course around the difficult, figure-of-eight circuit. When, three fences out, the exhausted Mandarin broke down in one of his forelegs, the chance of victory looked to have gone. Winter, though, urged him into the lead 100 yards out and managed to hold off the French horse Lumino by a head. John Oaksey, the jockey and journalist, wrote: 'I have never seen a comparable feat, never expect to – and can only thank God I was there.' Winter was unnecessarily gruff for some tastes, although his friends said this was a result of shyness. What was beyond reproach was his integrity, which stood out in a sport that had more than its fair share of rum characters.

RANDOLPH TURPIN
1928–1966

RANDOLPH TURPIN produced one of the most spectacular results in boxing history when he outfought Sugar Ray Robinson in London in 1951 to win the world middleweight title. The result briefly enriched but ultimately blighted what was to be a short life. Born in Leamington, Turpin was the third son of a British Guianian father and an English mother. His two brothers also boxed, but it was the skilful, awkward, solid-hitting Randolph who made the greatest impact. He was a successful amateur, becoming the first black fighter to win an ABA title. His early days as a professional were made difficult by domestic problems, including a custody battle with his first wife over their son, but these seemed to be behind him when he won the British middleweight title in October 1950. He added the European crown soon afterwards and it was decided he was now ready to take on Robinson, for years as bright a body as there was in the boxing firmament. Robinson arrived in London after a tour of Europe conducted in an open-topped pink Cadillac and accompanied by fifty-three suitcases. The 18,000 tickets for the fight at Earls Court sold out in three days. Turpin's crouching style baffled Robinson, who said he had no alibis for the defeat. When they met again sixty-four days later, however, he was ready for Turpin. The surprise of the first fight helped to attract a huge crowd of 61,000 to the Polo Grounds, New York. Although Turpin rallied after a slow start and opened a deep cut over Robinson's eye, he suffered a knockdown in the tenth. Turpin rose as the count reached seven only to receive even worse punishment and the referee stepped in. The crowd had sung 'For He's a Jolly Good Fellow' after the first Robinson fight and Turpin received £70,000 to defend his title, but the recognition and rewards started to destabilise him. He would have other successes, winning the British and Empire light-heavyweight titles, before returning to New York for another attempt at the world middleweight title, this time against Carl 'Bobo' Olson. He lost on points after his preparation was disrupted by a female acquaintance from the second Robinson fight. She later accused him of rape and assault, involving him in expensive and distressing court action. He was still only twenty-five but a fighter already on the slide. He retired in 1958 and, after tax problems added to his other woes, he shot himself.

ROGER BANNISTER
— 1929– —

A LIFETIME'S WORK devoted to medicine was overshadowed by the 3 minutes 59.4 seconds Roger Bannister took to win a race in Oxford on 6 May 1954. Running a mile in under four minutes was widely regarded as being as improbable as finding the unicorn, and Bannister, born in north London, did not seem particularly well qualified to turn myth into reality. For all his promise as a runner, his bookish personality marked him out more for a life of academic than athletic success. At school he overreached what sons of working-class parents were used to achieving in the 1940s and 1950s by winning a scholarship to Oxford. Although he kept up his athletics, and was good enough to run at the 1948 Olympics, he caused consternation when he declined a place to concentrate on training and medical studies. Critics believed his singular training methods, with sessions lasting less than an hour, did not tax him enough. These critics felt vindicated when he failed at the 1952 Olympics in Helsinki. He set out to prove himself after this, making his objective the first four-minute mile. In May 1954, by which time he was at medical school, his chance came at a meeting held at Iffley Road, Oxford, in which he represented the Amateur Athletic Association against his old university. Despite a gusting crosswind, his friends Christopher Chataway and Chris Brasher set the perfect pace, taking him through three-quarters of a mile in under three minutes. With 200 yards to go, Bannister kicked past Chataway to break the unbreakable record. Following the glittering coronation of the young Queen Elizabeth II and the British Mount Everest Expedition's conquest of the world's highest mountain a year earlier, it was another significant boost to British prestige abroad and a cause for rejoicing at home. Within forty-six days, Australia's John Landy lowered the record to 3 minutes 58.0 seconds. This set the scene for 'The Mile of the Century' when Bannister and Landy met later that summer in the British Empire Games in Vancouver. Bannister won it, passing Landy on one side as the Australian turned his head to the other to check his rival's position. Bannister, who retired soon afterwards, finished in 3 minutes 58.8 seconds; Landy 3 minutes 59.6 seconds. Bannister, who was knighted in 1975, combined a career in research with clinical practice as a neurologist before cutting back on his work after a serious car accident.

GRAHAM HILL
⟊ 1929–1975 ⟊

GRAHAM HILL went from driving a car for the first time to the world drivers' title in less than a decade. He was twenty-four before he turned over an engine and the first car he owned, a beaten-up 1929 Austin, had no brakes until he scraped together the necessary to install some. Driving a car that needed ingenuity rather than mechanical assistance to stop it was invaluable in developing the anticipation that served him so well on high-speed circuits. Hill was an exemplar of the adage that success comes only to those who want it badly enough. As is usually the case, this wanting proved to be a response to an inherent ability. His commitment to a sporting life took him first to rowing, hence the London Rowing Club colours on his helmet, and then, after paying five shillings to drive at Brands Hatch, to motor racing. As with Jim Clark, his confrère in elevating the reputation of British driving, Hill owed his start in grand prix racing to the Lotus chief Colin Chapman. But whereas the self-effacing Clark impressed Chapman with one brilliant drive, the more forceful but less gifted Hill did it over time after talking his way into a job in the Lotus workshops. Hill raced his first grand prix in 1958 and stayed with Lotus until 1960 when, frustrated by mechanical failures that he felt were holding him back, he switched to BRM. He won the world title with BRM in 1962 and, after returning to Lotus to team up with Clark, won it again in 1968 in the tragic aftermath of Clark's death. One measure of Hill's great skill as a racing driver was his success at Monaco, the most complex of all circuits where he won five times. He also completed a unique triple crown by combining Monaco success with victories in the Indianapolis 500 in a Lola-Ford in 1966 and Le Mans, with Henri Pescarolo, for Matra in 1972. His career went into decline after he broke both legs in a bad accident in the US Grand Prix at Watkins Glen in 1969 and he started to build his own team around the promising driver Tony Brise. In 1975, a twin-engined plane piloted by Hill crashed in fog while trying to land at Elstree airfield near London, killing Hill, Brise and four others on board. Hill was as relaxed and genial a man away from the track as he was tense and testy when it came to racing. His smooth good looks, complete with Clark Gable moustache that he first cultivated as a rebellious act in the Royal Navy, and dry wit, which he deployed with a professional's timing, made him a media favourite. But his one big stab at acting, in the film *Grand Prix*, was a salutary lesson in why racing drivers should stick to driving. Hill's son, Damon, carried on the family motor racing tradition by winning the world title in 1996.

STIRLING MOSS
1929–

STIRLING MOSS was more than just a racing driver, he was the embodiment of motor racing. Long after his fourteen years of competitive driving were over, his name resonated in the popular imagination even though he was never world champion. Petrified passengers and speed cops perpetuated his memory with the language-entering 'Who do you think you are, Stirling Moss?' He was the original insatiable enthusiast whose enthusiasm became his livelihood. No scholar – although he was smart enough not to follow his father into dentistry – he seemed cut out to do only one thing. And it did not matter what he was driving so long as it had a certain style and he could coax some speed out of it. He mastered all types of racing, particularly sportscar, prompting one specialist writer to suggest that if there had been a motor racing decathlon, Moss would have been uncatchable. He was born in London, into a sporting family. Both his parents liked racing, his father competed at Indianapolis, and his younger sister Pat was a high-grade showjumper and rally driver. His father bought him an old Austin Seven when he was nine so that he could drive it in the fields near their home. The price his parents had to pay for this early introduction to driving was having to curb his passion for a pursuit that would surely burn money rather than earn it. They tried, unsuccessfully, to divert him into the hotel business, waiting and night portering proving contrary to his talents. Moss was only eighteen when he started racing in 1948. He won ten out of fourteen races in his 497 cc Cooper, a car that his parents helped him buy on his eighteenth birthday. He had a number of notable years, high among them 1955 when, driving for Mercedes, he won his first grand prix, the British at Aintree, and scored the only win by a Briton in the Mille Miglia in Italy. In the British Grand Prix he beat the great Argentine Juan Fangio, although he was never quite sure whether Fangio had let him win in front of his home crowd. His victory in the Mille Miglia, a thousand miles over roads open to traffic, was widely regarded as his finest achievement, his time of 10 hours 7 minutes, at an average speed of 98 mph, being a record. The spirit in which Moss drove was never better illustrated than when in 1958 in the Portuguese Grand Prix he defended his rival Mike Hawthorne against a disqualification that would have cost him seven points. Hawthorne would beat Moss in that year's world championship by a single point. A serious accident at Goodwood in 1962, after which he was unconscious for twenty-eight days, ended his racing career. Moss was trenchant and single-minded in all things, which was one factor in the world title eluding him – although he won every grand prix worth winning and no one doubted his brilliance. Ferrari, for one, recognised his outstanding qualities and wanted to sign him, but Moss preferred to drive for British teams, however uncompetitive. For the effect this loyalty had on morale, domestic motor racing still owes him a huge debt of gratitude.

CLIFF MORGAN
1930–

CLIFF MORGAN embodied every young Welshman's longings with his special gifts as a rugby union player and his rich, euphonious voice. In the reduced, postwar years, Morgan's expansive performances for Cardiff, Wales and the British and Irish Lions pointed the way to a more interesting future, which he himself would be a part of as a major figure in broadcasting. Trebanog, a mining village in the Rhondda, remained his base for longer than it would have done had it not been for his formidable mother. She told the Wigan rugby league representatives who placed one thousand £5 notes and a postdated cheque for £2,500 on the family breakfast table that her twenty-two-year-old son was staying put. 'My mother believed in the security of village life,' Morgan said, 'that's why she stopped me going to Oxford University.' Morgan played his first game for Cardiff at eighteen and made his Wales debut in 1951, a month before his twenty-first birthday. He was a central figure in the Wales side who won the grand slam in 1952, the Wales and Cardiff teams who inflicted the only defeats in Britain on the 1953–4 All Blacks and on the 1955 Lions tour of South Africa. He also had a spell with the Irish team Bective Rangers, his influence being such that they were renamed the Morgan Rangers. Morgan called the 1955 Lions tour 'the best time of my life'. A second tenor in the Porth and District Choral Society, he brought zest and quality to the party's recreational interludes off the pitch; on it, he found the hard surfaces were the perfect platform for his running game. Perhaps his greatest performance was in the first Test of the drawn 2–2 series, an epic contest watched by 100,000 in Johannesburg. The Lions won 23–22 with Morgan scoring a brilliant try. In common with many talented players of his era, Morgan gave up rugby long before he might have done in the professional era. He was already being courted to captain the 1959 Lions to Australasia and Canada when in 1958 he retired because 'I couldn't afford to go on playing'. Morgan's fluency when a microphone came near him had been noted during his playing days and he slipped easily into a broadcasting career. Even a serious stroke when he was forty-one, which halted his career for eleven months, proved no more than a brief pause on his upward path. In 1981, as the BBC's head of outside broadcasts, the boy from Trebanog oversaw one of the biggest live operations in the Corporation's history, covering the wedding of Prince Charles and Lady Diana Spencer.

JOHN CHARLES
1931–2004

JOHN CHARLES chose football from a number of options to make what he could of himself, which turned out to be a great deal. Had he chosen Hollywood, he would have placed John Wayne in danger of being cast as the bad guy. Charles possessed rugged good looks and was scrupulously decent in all he did. When he played in Italy for Juventus, even the fans of city rivals Torino idolised him after an incident in a 1957–8 derby. After accidentally felling a Torino defender, Charles passed the ball out of play for a goal kick rather than try to take advantage of the scoring opportunity he had just created. A Juventus team-mate, Giampiero Boniperti, said of him: 'He was extraordinary, I would say from another world because of his human qualities.' As a footballer, he exceeded all other great players in the high standard he achieved both in defence and attack. His strength, energy, mobility, control with either foot and, particularly, his power in the air persuaded Leeds United, short of goals, to switch their outstanding young centre-half to centre-forward. He responded better than they could have hoped. Charles was playing in a public park when he was spotted by a Leeds scout. He played his first Football League match as a seventeen-year-old, picked at centre-half against Blackburn Rovers having filled right- and left-sided positions in the Leeds reserves. He was chosen by Wales in 1950, when still eighteen, and settled straightaway into the international game as an imposing defender. When the Leeds forwards stopped scoring, they were shown how by Charles, who contributed two goals in his second game up front. Although he returned to defence, he had placed the club in a quandary over where he should play. Charles himself solved it with his exceptional form when switched back to attack. He scored 42 goals in 1953–4, 12 more than the next highest scorer; and 38 in forty league games in 1956–7. This success meant Leeds would lose him, although they were compensated by the record fee of £65,000 that took him to Italy. Hitherto Continental clubs had regarded the north of England as a forbidding industrial area with equally grim teams and footballers. Charles's performances shone through and he rewarded Juventus with 93 goals in five seasons, helping the club to three league championships. While with Juventus, Charles guided Wales to their only World Cup finals. These were in Sweden in 1958, where Wales rose above modest expectations to reach a quarter-final against eventual champions Brazil. Charles missed the match through injury and Wales lost to a goal from Pelé. After Juventus, Charles went back to Leeds and then returned to Italy to play for Roma, but by now injuries had exposed him as mortal.

FRED TRUEMAN
⟶ 1931–2006 ⟵

FRED TRUEMAN was as close to the paradigm of a fast bowler as it is possible to imagine: disconcerting speed generated by an uncomplicated, flowing action that meant he was rarely injured. He had other attributes that the public admire in quicks: a feisty attitude and a rustic approach to batting that hardly made him the all-rounder he claimed to be but yielded 150 of his 981 Test runs in slogged sixes. His feistiness was occasionally crass, as it was at times on the 1953–4 tour of West Indies – although his reported remark to a local dignitary of 'Pass t' salt, Gunga Din' was never said – but was generally harmless and, when he played the Yorkshire working-class hero with style, could be amusing. 'Ay, lad – and I wasted it on thee,' was how Fiery Fred responded to one young university batsman who complimented him on the ball that had shattered his stumps. His inclination to play up to his place in the ranks, in a sport that had more representatives of

BEST OF BRITISH

FRED TRUEMAN

the officer class than most, helped to explain his brushes with the establishment, who became overly keen to punish him. He alone had his good-conduct bonus withheld after the West Indies tour, while his suspensions helped to limit him to sixty-seven Test caps. In fact it was the real officer class who facilitated Trueman's Test debut, his RAF superiors freeing him from national service duties to play against India at his home ground, Headingley, in 1952. He bowled frighteningly fast early on to contribute to a total of no run for four wickets. Trueman entered first-class cricket in 1949 and was a public figure from his first Test until his death. The apogee of his achievements was having Australia's Neil Hawke caught at slip at the Oval in 1964 to make him the first bowler to take 300 Test wickets. This was at the end of a great career, and although many have emulated him, few have matched the miserliness of 307 Test dismissals at 21.57 runs each. When Trueman was in his prime, Yorkshire were supreme, winning six county titles in the 1960s. He retired after the 1968 season in which he led Yorkshire to victory over the Australians at a time when counties and touring sides regarded their matches as serious contests. His work as a broadcaster – complete with the catchphrase, 'I don't know what's going off out there' – ensured that the colourful reputation he gained as a player was, if anything, enhanced. Trueman was fiercely protective of the cricket played in his era. When someone commented that in archive footage he did not appear to be as fast as later generations, he said this was simply because of the slowing-down effect of black-and-white images.

BILLY BOSTON
1934–

BILLY BOSTON was a charismatic rugby league winger who helped to revitalise interest in the sport. Crowds going to rugby league peaked in 1949–50 when a record 69.8 million paid to watch matches. The game's following then declined until it started to be televised in the 1950s – and no one attracted the cameras quite like Boston. A big man, whose mother was Irish and father Sierra Leonean, he could outpace sprightlier-looking rivals or confound them with one of the game's best side steps. Or he could simply use his strength to bulldoze through or fend off would-be tacklers. He broke numerous scoring records during his seventeen-year career, spent mostly at Wigan, ending with a tally of 571 tries. St Helens, Wigan's great rivals, responded to Boston's brilliance by investing in the South African winger Tom van Vollenhoven, who was blisteringly quick. Who was better? Wigan and Saints fans were still arguing half a century later. Criticism of portraying rugby league as a game played by cheery northerners was about to surface and was largely a reaction to the folksy com-mentaries of Eddie Waring on BBC Television. But Boston happily played his part, too. At Salford one day, with little to do on the wing, he ate a meat pie during play having been handed it by a spectator. In a very different interaction with

85

the crowd during a match at Hull, he stepped on to the terracing to seek out someone who shouted a racial insult. Unpardonably, race did not become an issue after Boston's treatment at the 1957 World Cup in Australia. When the rest of the team diverted to white-ruled South Africa to play promotional games, Boston flew home directly and alone to avoid creating a problem for the apartheid regime. Boston never forgot the slight of his team-mates going without him. Born and raised in the Cardiff melting pot of Tiger Bay, Boston was the sixth of eleven children. He played rugby union for Neath and, while doing national service, for the Royal Signals. It was after he scored six tries against the Welsh Guards in the Army Cup final in March 1953 that he signed for £3,000 to play rugby league for Wigan, who had sent four directors to watch the match at Aldershot. His first game for the A team attracted a crowd of more than 8,000 to Central Park. Still only nineteen, and having played just six club matches, he was selected for the Lions tour of Australasia in 1954. He made an immediate impact by scoring two tries in the second Test against Australia, which the Lions won. Boston played for Wigan until 1968 before finishing with two seasons at Blackpool where, now weighing more than 15 stone, he switched to the second row. After he retired, he remained a popular figure in Wigan as landlord of the Griffin. The beer was at its best when he remembered to turn the refrigerator back on, having switched it off at night because the noise kept his wife awake.

HENRY COOPER

PART SIX

DEATH AND GLORY
1934–1939

HENRY COOPER

1934–

HENRY COOPER's achievements in seventeen years of professional boxing were distilled into the split second it took his left hand to land on Cassius Clay's jaw on 18 June 1963. The punch was the quintessence of 'Enery's 'Ammer, the popular name for Cooper's left hook with the aitches dropped in deference to his south London accent. Cooper had the rare ability to hit from short range at lightning speed, which gave him a chance against the very best – and there would be none better than Cassius Clay. It was said of Cooper's left hook that it travelled fifteen times faster than a Saturn V rocket and landed with nearly three tons of force. Clay said Cooper hit him so hard 'even my ancestors in Africa felt it'. It was the first time Clay had been put on the canvas and Cooper would probably have won the fight at Wembley Stadium if the bell had not ended the fourth round moments later. Clay's wily cornerman Angelo Dundee admitted that, during the break, he pulled open a slight tear on his man's glove, which meant a new one had to be brought to the ring. This gave Clay time to recover and he stopped Cooper in the next round with a badly cut eye. Three years later, Clay, now known as Muhammad Ali and holder of the world title, beat Cooper again on cuts, this time in the sixth round. Cooper, who was twenty minutes older than his twin brother George, had 84 bouts as an amateur. He won the British light-heavyweight title in 1952 and during national service with the Royal Army Ordnance Corps – aka the Boxers' Battalion – he knocked out his company sergeant-major. He turned professional in 1954 and fought fifty-five times, his forty victories including twenty-seven inside the distance. He was British champion for most of his pro career, winning the Lonsdale belt outright, and he also held the European and Empire (later Commonwealth) titles. Cooper, who was small compared to the heavyweights who came after him, retired after a controversial defeat by Joe Bugner in 1971. The referee, Harry Gibbs, gave the British and Commonwealth title fight to Bugner by a quarter of a point, although most ringside observers made Cooper the winner. After boxing, Cooper made a good living as a TV pundit and from endorsing products. A tools company that bore his surname branded one of its products 'Henry's Hammer'. He also worked hard raising money for charity. Cooper, who had a salt-of-the-earth-Englishman image and was remarkably ingenuous for someone who lived by his fists, was knighted in 2000. He also shared with Lord Nelson and Lady Diana, among others, the accolade of being invoked by commentator Bjørge Lillelien in 1981 when Norway's footballers gave England a 'hell of a beating' in a World Cup qualifier.

PETER CRAVEN
1934–1963

PETER CRAVEN bore a passing resemblance to the actor James Dean. It was a bond that was tragically made a little less slender by Craven's death at the height of his considerable fame as a speedway rider. Craven was the kid brother who was attracted to his older sibling's sporting passion and went on to win the world title. He lost his life because he was unaffected by his celebrity and instinctively regarded 'never letting anyone down' as the right way to behave. Craven, a Liverpudlian, had a twin, Paul, who died when he was three, which is perhaps one reason why Peter drew so close to his big brother. Brian Craven introduced him to speedway racing, which had arrived in Britain from the United States, via Australia, in 1928. It proved such an instant success with spectators that Britain's first speedway league began the next year. The world championship arrived in 1936, with crowds of up to 90,000 packing Wembley in the 1950s. Craven crashed and was concussed when he first tried to ride a speedway bike, the difficult skill of 'broadsliding' through corners proving too great a physical challenge for the diminutive sixteen-year-old. His persistence led to his graduating to the Liverpool Chads team in division two of the National League in 1951. From then on, his mastery of the sport developed rapidly. The title of a biography, *Peter Craven: Wizard of Balance*, succinctly reflected his greatest strength even if its conciseness underplayed the problems of balancing an object as uncooperative as a revved-up bike. Craven moved to Belle Vue, top-scoring for the club in 1954 when he made twenty-four league appearances. In 1955, at only his second attempt, he confounded expectation by winning the world title with the formidable New Zealand pair of Ronnie Moore and Barry Briggs behind him. He remained at the forefront of the sport for the rest of his life, winning the title for a second time in 1962 in front of 62,000 at Wembley. In 1963, he failed to retain the title after suffering a heavy fall. Despite the effects of this spill and fatigue after a long season, he insisted on going to Edinburgh to ride in a meeting that many thought was nothing more than a high-profile friendly. He won three races brilliantly and then agreed to a 20-yard handicap in the final heat so that he could demonstrate his overtaking technique. He passed two riders before the engine of the bike in front of him seized. In trying to avoid a collision, he was hurled into the wooden safety fence and suffered fatal injuries.

BRIAN CLOUGH
⟞⟝ 1935–2004 ⟞⟝

BRIAN CLOUGH brought the football manager out of the dugout into the murky mainstream of public life. There had been plenty of banner managers before him, but none wrote his headlines throughout every section of the prints quite like self-styled 'Old Big 'Ead'. He was – among other things and in alphabetical order – an antagonist, bully, charmer, chivalrous knight, controversialist, devoted family man, exhibitionist, heavy drinker, pain in the butt, phrase-maker, polemicist, political activist, psychologist, punk philosopher, rascal and wonderfully warm human being. He was also a thunderingly good manager whose overstuffed list of achievements eclipsed a playing career that was winding up to be significant before a knee injury ended it. His 251 goals in 274 appearances for Middlesbrough and Sunderland spoke for themselves. In 1959, aged twenty-four, he won two England caps. Early on in his managerial career, which began at Hartlepool in 1965, he teamed up with Peter Taylor, a former goalkeeper who became Clough's coaching partner. They proved a perfect fit, if only because Taylor provided the silence into which Clough could pour his garrulousness. Clough's greatest coups were at Nottingham Forest and Derby County, where his trick of turning modest East Midlands clubs into Football League champions – and, in Forest's case, European Cup winners in 1979 and 1980 – looked little short of alchemy. In fact, Clough's coaching methods were devoid of trickery. Typically, he would tell his strikers in training, 'Hit the target' – and do no more than repeat this directive ad nauseam. Off the field, he would build up or deflate egos as he saw fit, which he could do sensitively or with all the guile of a starched nanny dealing with a recalcitrant child. His time in management had its troughs and omissions, including a dalliance with Leeds in 1974 that lasted forty-four days, a failure to win the FA Cup and an unfulfilled ambition to get the England job, for which he was interviewed in 1977 but thought too volatile to be risked. Among many eccentric Clough moments was an incident in 1989 when he cuffed a fan who ran on to the pitch and then, a few days later, kissed him in front of the TV cameras. On another occasion, he invited the Forest team to drink as much alcohol as they could on the eve of a big match as a way of bonding. Perhaps the eighteen years Clough spent at Forest were too many, the team's fortunes and the manager's drinking travelling, exponentially, in opposite directions. He retired from management in 1993, and died of cancer eleven years later.

LESTER PIGGOTT
1935–

LESTER PIGGOTT set a standard for the ruthless pursuit of success that few have come close to matching, whatever the sport. His passion was horseracing and fellow jockeys, trainers, owners, spectators and horses all experienced the force of

Piggott's pathological desire to be first. This might have been no more than the piercing coldness of one of his looks when his mind was focused on winning; or it might have been the flesh-searing slap of a whip such as Roberto experienced when Piggott drove him to a short-head victory over Rheingold in the 1972 Derby. He took risks, too, and explained: 'You can't do two things, do your best to win all the time, and be careful all the time.' The upshot was the longest-lasting career of any athlete in the twentieth century. It began in 1948, while he was still only twelve, and ended just short of his sixtieth birthday in 1995. With his familiar riding style, short stirrups and well-elevated posterior putting a premium on perfect balance, he rode 4,493 winners on the flat, 20 over hurdles in Britain, and more than 1,200 in twenty-six countries outside the UK. His wins included a record thirty Classics, nine of them in the Derby. The authorities did not always take a lenient view of his methods. In 1954, soon after he had become, at eighteen, the youngest winner of the Derby on Never Say Die, he received a ban of six months, later halved, for 'complete disregard of the rules of racing and safety of other jockeys'. There were other infringements that, despite the penalties, added to Piggott's reputation as a horseman. In mid-race at Deauville, he grabbed the whip from Alain Lequeux's hand after he had dropped his own. He used the occasion to show off his dry wit, suggesting what had in fact happened was that Lequeux, realising he was beaten, had handed him the whip as an act of comradeship. At Sha Tin in Hong Kong, he pushed away the head of another horse with his hand while racing at speed. Later in life, Piggott was targeted by more serious law enforcers and in 1987 received a three-year prison sentence for tax offences, for which he was stripped of his OBE. He was released on parole after 366 days and in 1990, approaching his fifty-fifth birthday, made a comeback. Piggott, who became the oldest British flat jockey, took two weeks to prove wrong those who doubted his ability to ride as brilliantly as he had in the past. In the view of many, his surge to victory on Royal Academy in the 1990 Breeders' Cup Mile at Belmont Park, New York, made his comeback the most remarkable in sporting history. He rode his last winner in October 1994 and quit riding for good in 1995.

JIM CLARK
1936–1968

JIM CLARK drove racing cars thrillingly – and lived the rest of his life as barnstormingly as a pensioner going for an afternoon spin. While the world regarded the shy Scotsman as an exceptionally gifted driver who kept a few sheep, Clark saw himself as a livestock farmer from the Borders who also raced cars. He hated the ballyhoo of the grand prix circus, even the subdued ballyhoo of the 1960s. Privately educated at Loretto School near Edinburgh, Clark took to driving cars as others take to playing musical instruments. It was said he could stand a saloon car on two wheels while taking a corner and still have it under finger-tip control. He ignored parental opposition to start competitive driving when he entered his own Sunbeam-Talbot in local road rallies and hill climbs. He graduated to the Border Reivers team when he was twenty-one, smoothly negotiating the transition to the far meatier challenge of driving such marques as Jaguar and Porsche. The break that gained him elevation to motor racing's most rarefied company came on Boxing Day 1958 when he impressed Colin

Chapman by finishing second to him in one of Chapman's own Lotus Elites. It was as a result of this performance that Chapman and Clark joined up to become Formula One's commanding presence. Clark took over as Lotus team leader in 1962 and in 1963, aged twenty-seven, was the youngest winner of the world drivers' title, dominating the championship in the Lotus 25 with 7 wins in 10 grands prix. The car's unreliability was the only factor that denied Clark more championships, although he won the world title again in 1965. The same year he also won the Indianapolis 500, the first European to do so for forty-five years, in a Lotus that Chapman designed specifically for the race. His performance in the 1967 Italian Grand Prix at Monza became the standard by which all other great drives would be judged. He lost an entire lap having a wheel changed but counterattacked superbly to regain the lead. Agonisingly, his car, low on fuel, spluttered and coasted over the finishing line in third place. Clark's death in an accident at Hockenheim on 7 April 1968 raised a number of questions, including: why was he bothering with a Formula Two race on a circuit he had not previously driven? (The answer was partly to do with a contractual obligation to a Lotus supplier.) There was also the question of why he lost control coming out of an easy bend. The likeliest explanation was a deflating rear tyre, although nothing was proved. Clark raced in seventy-two grands prix, started from pole thirty-three times and won twenty-five. He was absurdly modest and genuinely bemused by his success, which led to the line for which he was most remembered: 'I really don't understand why everyone else is so slow.' After the crash that killed him, fellow-driver Chris Amon asked: 'If it could happen to him, what chance do the rest of us have?'

DUNCAN EDWARDS
——✦ 1936–1958 ✦——

DISTINGUISHING HYPERBOLE from rational assessment is difficult when considering Duncan Edwards's short life, but the evidence of eyewitnesses and statisticians is too over-whelming for there to be any doubt that he was outstanding. The debate is only over how outstanding he was. Edwards was twenty-one when he died. He had fought for fifteen days to survive kidney damage, the worst of the injuries he suffered in the plane crash on 6 February 1958 that killed seven of his Manchester United team-mates. By then, Edwards had already played 151 times for United and 18 times for England. He is usually classified as a left-sided midfield player, but his commanding 6 foot 3 inch presence, strength, stamina and range of skills, from shooting powerfully with either foot to distributing long, accurate passes to dribbling with a natural ball player's control, meant he filled many more positions. He was destined to be a pivotal figure for club and country. Walter Winterbottom, the manager who made him England's youngest international for more than seventy years when he picked him in 1955 at eighteen years 183 days, said: 'It was in the character and spirit of Duncan Edwards that I saw the true revival of British football.' That first international was against Scotland at Wembley, where Edwards played with poise and without a hint of nerves in a 7–2 victory. Born in Dudley, Worcestershire, Edwards appeared on the radar of leading clubs while still in his early teens. He met all the criteria of a Busby Babe, the name given to the youthful recruits enrolled by the Manchester United manager Matt Busby because the club were too impoverished to sign established players. United

BEST OF BRITISH

DUNCAN EDWARDS

duly won the race for his signature and took him on as a full-time professional on 1 October 1953, Edwards's seventeenth birthday. By then he had already set the first of his youngest-ever records by appearing in the Football League First Division aged sixteen years 185 days. Edwards's rise to meet, time and again, the greatest expectations placed on him ended in Munich after the aeroplane in which the United team were travelling slithered across slush and snow into a perimeter fence. Initially, he was thought to have a good chance of pulling through but the damage to his kidneys was too severe. His grave in Dudley remains a place of pilgrimage and he is depicted in a stained-glass window in a local church.

JOS NAYLOR
1936–

JOS NAYLOR ran because he loved to and because he loved the countryside in which he ran. The steep fells of the Lake District in north-west England were where he lived, farmed sheep and did most of his running. The stamina he exhibited in fell races and paced endurance runs gained him a world-wide reputation. Chris Brasher, the 1956 Olympic steeplechase champion, wrote: 'I have always believed that Jos is the toughest runner in Britain, which inevitably makes him the toughest runner in the world because no other nation has the depth of talent in those events that pull the stamina out of a man's heart.' Naylor, spare and weather-beaten, showed no inclination to test himself in the major marathons in which he would almost certainly have been successful and later in life he agreed that he had not fully exploited his potential. As he understated it, endurance running was simply a matter of 'determination and holding the pace'. He said that his farming made it difficult for him to train as hard as might be necessary; that it was only by racing and working that he managed to stay fit. The greatest demonstration of his fitness came on a hot day in July 1975 when, running from early one morning to early the next, he conquered 72 Lake District peaks in 23 hours 11 minutes. He covered 105 miles and scaled an aggregate of 37,000 feet, 8,000 feet more than the height of Everest, to fulfil his wish to set 'a record that will last'. A song written to celebrate this started, 'Jos Naylor of Wasdale/ Greatest fell runner of our time' – and one national news-paper reported his achievement under the headline: 'He's pushing forty, runs on his wife's rock cakes – and has just achieved the most astonishing physical feat you can imagine'. He had back problems as a young man. After visiting scores of specialists, he was advised by a surgeon to have two discs removed, which he did and the problems went away. The surgeon also told Naylor that he had the physique to be 'an athlete in a million'. This physique held up so well after the operation that on his seventieth birthday in 2006 he set out at 2 a.m. to run over 70 fell tops in just 21 hours, on another boiling July day. He covered more than 50 miles and climbed more than 25,000 feet.

GORDON BANKS
⟶ 1937- ⟶

GORDON BANKS named his autobiography *Banks of England*, a nice pun on an inestimable goalkeeper who may not have been quite as secure as a strongroom door, but near enough. It was not always the case. Starting out, he let in 15 goals in two games for a Yorkshire League side and was promptly sacked. His apprenticeships with a coal merchant and on building sites seemed to point the way to his livelihood. This changed in 1955 after a scout recognised the seventeen-year-old's potential and signed him for Chesterfield of the Third Division North. Implausibly, considering all he achieved, Banks never played for one of the major clubs. In 1959, he moved to Leicester City for £7,000; then in 1967 he went to Stoke City for £52,000, despite Liverpool's known interest in him. Banks is credited with having modernised goalkeeping, expanding its scope beyond the rudimentary task of stopping shots. His international career started inauspiciously in 1963 when England lost 2-1 to Scotland in Alf Ramsey's second game as manager. Ramsey knew enough of Banks's worth, though, to keep him in the side. The 1966 and 1970 World Cup finals would mark Banks out as a goalkeeper fit for consideration as number one among No. 1s. When England won the World Cup in 1966, they played 443 minutes before Banks let in a goal, Eusebio's penalty for Portugal in the semi-final. Banks rated this as the best of the seventy-three internationals in which he played: 'The football has never in my experience been surpassed.' In the final against West Germany, he let in two, half as many as went in (or almost went in) at the other end. Banks's greatest match was against Brazil at the 1970

World Cup in Mexico. England lost 1–0, but Banks's save from Pele's header is now widely regarded as one of the most sublime moments in sport. Pele screamed 'Goal' after he rose above the ball and, with considerable force, angled it perfectly to bounce up into the net by Banks's right post. Somehow Banks intercepted the ball with his right hand after it hit the ground and flicked it clear. Illness kept Banks out of the quarter-final against West Germany and England's defence of the World Cup foundered. Banks lost the sight in his right eye after a road accident in 1972, effectively ending his career. He kept 35 clean sheets for England and was Fifa's Goalkeeper of the Year six times.

BERYL BURTON
1937–1996

BERYL BURTON's exploits as a cyclist undermined the idea that men's endurance events were too daunting for women. Long before the Olympics allowed female athletes to run over distances such as the marathon or 10,000 metres – or compete in any cycling events – Burton showed time and again that although women might not be as strong as men they could match them for stamina and the guts to keep going. She was pre-eminent in women's cycling in Britain and in certain world events for more than quarter of a century. The longevity of this domination in such a demanding sport may never be matched. An amateur 12-hour time trial in her native Yorkshire in 1967 was the event in which Burton convinced all but the most misogynistic sceptics that women were as durable as men. In that trial, Mike McNamara set a British

BEST OF BRITISH

BERYL BURTON

men's record of 276.52 miles, while Burton covered 277.25 miles. This added almost 27 miles to her previous best and made her the first woman to break a men's British record. As she passed McNamara, the men and women having started separately, she slowed to offer him a liquorice, which he accepted. Burton had her first race in 1954 and continued to compete until a few weeks before her death when she suffered heart failure during a training ride. Throughout her life, despite all the acclaim, she regarded herself primarily as a club cyclist. One of her greatest pleasures was riding with her daughter, Denise, which they did as members of the British team in the world road race championship. Her 5 pursuit and 2 road world titles would have been many more had the current range of events existed in her time. She sacrificed the chance to win more road race championships by refusing to compromise her aggressive pace-setting tactics, which left her vulnerable in sprint finishes. Despite this she won 122 national titles and 7 world championships. Burton was an improbable candidate to achieve what she did. She was a sickly child, suffering a disorder of the central nervous system and rheumatic fever, which confined her to hospital and a convalescent home for fifteen months. For a while, she was paralysed down one side. In her riding career, she was dismissive of injuries. These included a broken right leg and shoulder and in 1978 cuts to her face that needed fifty-six stitches. She did stop riding during pregnancy, but that was for only three months when she could not squeeze behind the handlebars.

BOBBY CHARLTON
1937–

BOBBY CHARLTON neither looked nor acted the part of the consummate footballer he was. He lost his hair prematurely but tried to pretend otherwise by growing long strands that he laid over the bald area. These flapped like untied bootlaces when he ran around. When football started to turn sexy in the 1960s, he preferred a cup of tea and a cigarette to more exotic options. But this understatedness helped him cope with the pressure that being such a widely recognised figure exerted on him. He claimed he made his England debut in 1958, the year he survived the Munich air crash, only because the selectors felt sorry for him and he downplayed the goal against Mexico with which he vitalised England's run towards winning the 1966 World Cup. 'I just banged it,' he said. Charlton was brought up in the Northumberland mining village of Ashington, where pretension was a crime. Football was in the family. His brother Jackie played for Leeds and was a team-mate when England won the World Cup; 'Wor' Jackie Milburn, the Newcastle United and England centre-forward, was an uncle. Charlton joined Manchester United as a school-boy and made his debut aged eighteen in 1956. He started on the left before creating a niche for himself as a deep-lying centre forward. Unusual for the time, such positioning was possible only because of the smooth and devastating acceleration with which, in a matter of strides – and while remaining perfectly balanced – he created the space to deliver a fearsome shot from distance. Charlton was flung forty yards clear when the plane bringing Manchester United home from a European Cup tie in Belgrade skidded off the runway after a stop in Munich. Seven of the United team were killed. An eighth, Duncan Edwards, died later from his injuries. Charlton escaped with a cut head. He played in the FA Cup final for which United so improbably qualified at the end of the season and was the unflappable presence around which Matt Busby, once he had recovered from the severe injuries he suffered in the crash, rebuilt United into the team who won the 1968 European Cup. Charlton scored United's fourth goal in the 4–1 final victory over Benfica. He played 106 times for England, went to 4 World Cups and scored a record 49 goals for his country. Alf Ramsey, the England manager, described him as the linchpin of the team, which made it hardly surprising that their defence of the World Cup in 1970 fell apart when Ramsey removed Charlton in the quarter-final against West Germany. Perhaps, unlike his brother Jack, he was too gentle to survive in the world of management, but he retained his links with football as a director of Manchester United and as a committeeman for Fifa, the world game's governing body. He was knighted in 1994, roughly a quarter of a century later than he should have been.

ROY OF THE ROVERS
⟶ c.1937 ⟵

ROY OF THE ROVERS, the only Englishman to score a hat-trick in the first half of a European Cup final, soared above his flesh-and-blood equivalents as an inspirational force. No matter that Roy Race was a figment of the comic-book era, the Melchester Rover with the 'KPOWWWW' left foot, Race's Rocket, fired millions of youngsters to strive as they would never have done if he had not existed, which he did most graphically. Roy was devised in 1954 for the *Tiger* comic when the editor asked writer Frank Pepper to create a football hero. Soon afterwards the artist Joe Colquhoun assumed the writing and drawing duties, later to be replaced by Paul Trevillion, as Roy set off on a dazzling run through the years and over the football pitches of the world. Alf Leeds, a scout for Melchester Rovers, spotted Roy playing for a youth club and his career soared inexorably. He graduated through Rovers' youth and A sides to make his first-team debut in 1955, with two goals in a 3–3 draw. He progressed to being the Rovers captain, leading a side whose successes were commensurate with those of a superstar footballer. Roy played for and managed England and also went into club management, with Melchester and the Italian side AC Monza. Several times the end of *Roy of the Rovers* seemed nigh, either because of the fortunes of the publications in which he appeared or as a result of the lurid imaginations of the creators themselves. Roy was shot in 1982 and his playing career was ended in 1993 when his left foot was amputated after a helicopter crash. The launch of an official website in 1999 kept the legend going. Roy of the Rovers, whose name was frequently invoked by journalists trying to convey the sense of an improbable feat, was the most famous of a host of cartoon sportsmen. Others included Billy Dane, whose modest ability was transformed by a pair of boots that once belonged to 'Dead Shot' Keen; Alf Tupper, the 'Tough of the Track', hard-as-nails athlete; Wilson of the Wizard, born in 1795 but still going strong in the twentieth century when he ran a mile, across country, in three minutes; and Billy Whizz, who was not an athlete as such but as a boy could run amazingly fast – he provided the 2003 World Cup-winning England rugby player Jason Robinson with his nickname. As with all extraordinary characters, Roy was widely parodied. There was Billy the Fish in *Viz* and Lenin of the Rovers on radio, while *Private Eye*, the satirical magazine, delighted in running Roy of the Rovers parodies in response to the latest football scandal.

TOM SIMPSON
1937–1967

TOM SIMPSON died trying to be as competitive in the multi-stage Tour de France as he was in the much shorter cycling classics. His putative last words, 'Put me back on my bike', uttered after he collapsed close to the summit of Mont Ventoux, near Carpentras, tuned out to be the invention of a journalist. They did, though, accurately reflect the attitude of a rider who was, as some had long suspected, recklessly brave. Simpson died soon after collapsing for a second time from the combination of intense heat, whose effects were exacerbated by limitations on how much riders were allowed to drink, exhaustion, stimulants and alcohol. Two tubes of amphetamines and an empty one were found in a pocket of his racing top, while his blood was laced with brandy. The manner of his death did little to diminish him in the eyes of the public, who were not yet used to regular drug-taking scandals and saw what Simpson did as a mark of his bravery rather than cynicism. Regardless of what he ingested, Simpson was an exceptional road racer, an outsider capable of mixing it with the very best from the sport's heartland. Born in the coalmining community of Haswell, County Durham, Simpson moved to France in 1959 – he would later settle in Ghent, Belgium, where he was made a freeman – after an impressive amateur career. After arriving in Brittany, he won local amateur races and within three months gained a profes-

sional contract. He was the first Briton to wear the race leader's yellow jersey in the Tour de France in 1962, but relinquished it after a day, although he did go on to finish sixth overall. He made his name by winning classics such as the Tour of Flanders (1961), Bordeaux–Paris (1963), Milan–San Remo (1964) and Tour of Lombardy (1965). In 1965, he also became the first British holder of the world professional road race title, noting soon after he crossed the line that his badly worn rear tyre was on the point of bursting. Well known and well regarded in Britain, he was hugely admired on the Continent. The French called him the Major and, despite his working-class background, Simpson willingly submitted to being photographed with bowler hat and brolly. His death on 13 July on the thirteenth stage of the Tour de France was as big a story in his adopted countries as it was in Britain. Despite the involvement of drugs, British cyclists paid for a granite monument to be erected at the spot where Simpson died. A plaque added thirty years later read: 'There is no mountain too high. Your daughters Jane and Joanne, July 13 1997'.

HARVEY SMITH
1938–

HARVEY SMITH was showjumping's class warrior who took the sport away from the genteelly nurtured and gave it to a much wider audience. To say the Yorkshire builder's son did it single-handed is, in one very real sense, entirely accurate. The televised V-sign he flashed at Douglas Bunn, the autocratic owner of Hickstead, in 1971 did more for his and showjumping's popularity than he could possibly have imagined at the time. Following a row with Bunn and other officials of the Sussex course earlier in the day, Smith made the gesture from the saddle after winning the British Showjumping Derby. Initially, Bunn, who described Smith's behaviour as disgusting, ruled that he should lose his £2,000 prize and be disqualified. This merely added impetus to the story and under popular pressure, and with Smith protesting, unconvincingly, that it was a victory sign, the stewards rescinded the punishment. Smith was now the country's first celebrity showjumper and the sport's profile reached an elevated level that lasted until he faded from the scene. Smith's reputation was not solely based on a hand gesture. As well as being irascible, irreverent and irritating, he was an outstanding, self-taught horseman, even if his style was as rough-edged as he was. He liked to say: 'I just sits on 'em and pulls the strings.' Smith first came to public notice aged nineteen when, on his £40 horse Farmer's Boy, he made an immediate impact at the 1958 Royal International Show in London. For the next thirty years, his performances and achievements were closely followed by a far wider constituency than showjumping had ever previously commanded. Although success at Olympic Games and world championships eluded him, he was consistently Britain's best performer in the Nations Cup, exceeding all other members of the team with thirty-one victories. Smith, some times referred to as 'Heathcliff on horseback', made a lucrative living on the professional circuit. He attracted sponsors who appreciated that his personality was one the public connected with far more readily than those from the sport's grander wing. Later, he tried to relaunch himself as a singer and a wrestler. He made his wrestling debut in front of 1,300 spectators at the Royal Hall, Harrogate, against Cockey Kaye, the 'Lancashire Thunderbolt', in a bout billed as the 'Battle of the Pennines'. Smith wore a velvet robe with a big V embroidered on the back, emphasising just how important to him that two-fingered salute had been.

ALEX MURPHY
1939–

ALEX MURPHY was a perfectly balanced rugby league player with as formidable a belief in his ability as that ability was formidable. He was also endlessly controversial. He must have attracted more unambiguous adjectives than anyone who has played or coached the game, including this necessarily limited selection: abrasive, arrogant, cocksure, cunning, indomitable and super-confident. There were a number of ambiguous ones, too – such as shrewd. Murphy anecdotes are plentiful. He was said to have won the 1966 Challenge Cup final for St Helens by deliberately playing offside so that Wigan, without a specialist hooker, would concede possession at the ensuing scrum. In 1971, by which time he was player-coach at Leigh, he was accused of having the Leeds captain Syd Hynes sent off in Leigh's unexpected victory in the Challenge Cup final. 'People said I winked when I was on the stretcher,' Murphy said, reacting to the charge he had feigned injury from a headbutt. 'Well, I might have blinked but I didn't wink.' It was reckoned he caused the drop goal's reduction to one point because he overused it. Even without the shenanigans, Murphy would have left a vivid mark on the game. He was a scrum-half exceptionally quick of foot and wit. At school in St Helens, he played in the senior team at the age of ten. His hometown club were so worried that others might sneak in for him that they secured his signature moments after midnight on his sixteenth birthday, having first taken him to a secret location. He widened the breadth of his playing experience when representing the RAF at rugby union during national service. It was claimed, possibly by him, that he was responsible for finally making the youngest branch of the armed forces competitive with the Army and Navy. He frequently played union for the RAF and league for St Helens in the same week. In 1958, he succeeded Billy Boston as the youngest player to go on a Lions tour of Australasia and was hailed even by the never easily impressed Australians after his key role in winning the second Test when the Lions were reduced to eleven fit men. He further enhanced his reputation on the Lions' 1962 tour Down Under. His career lasted from 1958 until 1975 and he won rugby league's trophy of trophies, the Challenge Cup, as captain with each of his three clubs, St Helens, Leigh and Warrington. He was less lauded as a coach, his reputation never recovering from St Helens' 27–0 trashing by Wigan in the 1989 Wembley final. In retirement, he did BBC commentaries and wrote newspaper columns, one of them under the unironic heading 'Murphy's Mouth'.

MARY PETERS
1939–

MARY PETERS's greatest achievement, winning the pentathlon at the 1972 Olympics in Munich, was framed by violence: the Troubles at home in Northern Ireland and, two days after her victory, the slaughter that followed Palestinian terrorists breaking in to the Israel team's accommodation. To those who took notice, Peters provided a small but uplifting example of the less monstrous possibilities of human endeavour. A generous-spirited, friendly woman, Peters, who would later devote herself to community and charitable causes, had a yen for hard training and a lust for competition. This would see her confound expectation by beating Heidi Rosendahl, the formidable, spring-heeled West German athlete who had already won the long jump gold medal coming in to the pentathlon and was expected to be too good for Peters, who was thirty-three. Peters had finished fourth in the pentathlon at the 1964 Olympics and her last chance of winning gold

BEST OF BRITISH

MARY PETERS

apparently disappeared when an ankle injury made her uncompetitive at the 1968 Games. After the first day's competition in Munich, Peters's jolly demeanour, which would not have been out of place behind the beer pumps of a Belfast bar, provided the highlight when she ran around the stadium blowing kisses to the crowd after achieving a personal best of 1.82 metres in the high jump. It seemed an unnecessary waste of energy, especially as Rosendahl was particularly strong at the two events on the second day, the long jump and 200 metres. Rosendahl set a world record points' tally for the pentathlon when she won the 200 in 22.96 seconds, but she held it for only 1.12 seconds – the time it took for Peters to follow her across the line and raise the record by a mere 10 points to 4,801. One tenth of a second slower and Rosendahl's record would have stood. Peters was born in Liverpool and moved to Belfast aged eleven when her insurance broker father was transferred there. She embraced the city as her home, training in a heavily fortified gym, and refused to be daunted by the sectarian violence. Her Olympic gold-medal success was applauded by all factions and her tireless work raising money for new facilities culminated in the opening of Belfast's Mary Peters Track in 1975.

JACKIE STEWART
1939–

JACKIE STEWART stood out as a motor racing champion who dared to make safety a priority in a sport that had quietly prided itself on rewarding those who dared to do the opposite. What the Scot lost through prudence he more than made up for through the exquisitely smooth driving that won him three Formula One world championships. Stewart, born in 1939 into a family steeped in motorsport, was nearly put off fast cars when his brother Jimmy was badly injured in a crash at Le Mans in 1955. Mindful that his parents were worried about their second son's safety, he turned to his other sporting passion to try to win a place on Britain's clay-pigeon shooting team for the 1960 Olympics. He narrowly failed after under-performing at the final trials. In 1963, having returned to motor racing, he impressed the influential Ken Tyrrell when, in testing, he consistently returned faster times than the established Formula One driver Bruce McClaren. Stewart thrashed the opposition when he drove for Tyrrell in a Cooper-BMC in Formula Three, but he did not get a chance in F1 until 1965, when he moved to BRM. Stewart's attitude towards motor racing changed radically as a result of two dramatic events in 1966. First, he had cruel luck in his debut drive in the Indianapolis 500, breaking down when more than a lap ahead with eight laps to go; then he crashed in a rainstorm in the Belgian Grand Prix at Spa-Francorchamps. From then on, he was fastidious in his preparation for races and restless in his pursuit of better safety for drivers. At Spa, his team-mate Graham Hill had to use spanners from a spectator's toolkit to free him. The ambulance took more than half an hour to arrive and was further delayed on its way to the local hospital when the driver got lost. 'It was ridiculous,' said Stewart. He teamed up again with Tyrrell in 1968 when he produced perhaps the greatest drive of a career that was marked by exceptional performances. Against his better judgement, after Tyrrell convinced him the newly designed wet-weather tyres would be effective, Stewart took part in the German Grand Prix in appalling conditions. He led by 9 seconds after the first lap and, maintaining a control on the waterlogged surface that none of the others could match, won by 4 minutes. Stewart's devotion to the fine detail of every aspect of racing, from his own physical conditioning to the setting-up of his cars, saw him carry off his first world title in 1969, when he won 6 of the 11 grands prix in the Matra MS80. He won the title again in 1971 and 1973 when the combination of his own excellence and Tyrrell's car design was all powerful. After the fatal crash of his team-mate François Cevert in practice for the last race of 1973, the US Grand Prix, Stewart pulled out and retired. It would have been his hundredth F1 race. But he remained dedicated to introducing the measures that would in time make the sport remarkably safe considering its intrinsic dangers. He also formed his own team in the 1990s, winning one grand prix in 1999 before selling to Ford. He was knighted in 2001.

BOBBY MOORE

PART SEVEN

THEIR FINEST HOUR
1940–1955

GEOFFREY BOYCOTT
1940–

GEOFFREY BOYCOTT used immense willpower to produce results that comfortably exceeded what most sportsmen with his gifts would have settled for. Socially awkward but hugely ambitious, he found cricket suited the single-minded – some preferred selfish – streak in his personality. One of the many Boycott anecdotes, doubtless apocryphal, concerned the batting partner who met him mid-pitch to say he had sussed the secret of the bowler's 'mystery' ball. Boycott's response was that he had too, but had been keeping it to himself. Born in Fitzwilliam, Yorkshire, Boycott always protested that his childhood was a happy one despite his father's ill health caused by a coal-mining accident. He made his debut for Yorkshire as an opening batsman in 1962 and for England two years later. His 146, with 78 runs in boundaries, in the 1965 Gillette Cup final was one of the most exhilarating innings ever played in domestic one-day competitions. In due course, though, he curtailed free-flowing strokes, relying instead on risk-free shots that would earn him the sort of average on which he knew his career would be judged. In later life, when established as a commentary-box guru, he would support his view of a player by saying: 'Look at his average. The figures don't lie.' A batting average being runs divided by the number of times out, he was as dogged in defending his wicket as he was in making big scores; it is unlikely any batsman felt as woebegone at being dismissed as Boycott. The emphasis on self rebounded at times, notably when the selectors dropped him after he batted 573 minutes for 246 against India in 1967. In 1978, his dilatoriness led to a team-mate deliberately running

BEST OF BRITISH

GEOFF BOYCOTT

him out in a Test in New Zealand. Boycott's wider popularity suffered when he absented himself from thirty Tests apparently in a fit of pique after his being passed over as England captain. In the final reckoning, though, Boycott's own barometer of evaluation, cold statistics, spoke up for him: an average of 47.72 in 108 Tests and 151 first-class centuries. In 1977, when he returned for England against Australia, he showed an old trouper's sense of timing by making his 100th first-class century in front of a Headingley crowd who needed no persuading to forgive him his trespasses. Boycott's forward stroke epitomised his earnest approach, the big left pad thrust out a full stride and his head held low in close attendance. In attack Boycott restricted himself to strokes he knew best, notably the back-foot punch through the covers and the on-drive. After he retired, Boycott stayed in the headlines. He fought cancer and was involved in an unsavoury court case over an assault on a girlfriend before re-establishing his popularity as an assertive analyst for newspapers and broadcasters.

DENIS LAW
1940–

FOOTBALL TRANSFORMED Denis Law from gawky-looking kid to a man who comfortably wore the nickname The King, an unironic link to another entertainer of the 1950s and 1960s. Law's ability to shimmy and swivel in Manchester was as compelling as Elvis Presley's to do something similar in Memphis. It would have been hard to imagine when the scrawny, bespectacled seventeen-year-old turned up at Huddersfield Town in 1957 straight from school in Aberdeen, where, the youngest of seven children, he had been brought up in a council tenement. On the pitch, his awkwardness mutated into a rare facility for the game, particularly scoring goals. He could jump preternaturally high for a small man and, once up there, could head with stinging force. His skill with the ball at his feet was even more impressive. He maintained a tight control no matter how uneven the surface and had a nought-to-top-speed acceleration that left much bigger defenders standing like traffic bollards. Activating Law's renowned temper was, for a while, by far the most reliable way of stopping him. Law moved on to Manchester City and then Torino, where he was never really happy with the ultra-defensive play. Manchester United signed him for £116,000 and were repaid by Law's consistent brilliance. His goal-scoring acumen was a major contributor to United's winning the 1964–5 league title, their first since the 1958 Munich air crash, and regaining it in 1966–7. By 1968, Law had developed a chronic knee injury that kept him out of that year's European Cup final. Law was a proud Scot who distinguished himself with a record 30 goals in 55 internationals. He spent the afternoon on which England won the World Cup final in 1966 on the golf course. His round went badly and when he returned to the clubhouse to hear the result he flung aside his clubs and snorted: 'That makes my day.' He exacted revenge of a sort by scoring in Scotland's 3–2 win over England less than a year after their World Cup win. In 1973, he returned on a free transfer to Manchester City, where his back-heeled goal against Manchester United confirmed their relegation at the end of the 1973–4 season. He did not celebrate the goal, knowing its likely consequence, and walked off head bowed when he was substituted straight afterwards. The goal turned out to be his last kick in club football. He appeared for Scotland in the final stages of the 1974 World Cup in West Germany, but was disappointed to be dropped for the Brazil match after playing in the 2–0 win over Zaire.

WILLIE JOHN MCBRIDE
⟩———⟨ 1940– ⟩———⟨

WILLIE JOHN MCBRIDE found accommodation for his most imposing attributes on the Lions rugby union visit to Southern Africa in 1974. Big and brave and a leader to the marrow, McBride, from Ballymena in Northern Ireland, needed each of these assets on a tour of brutal intensity. If refusing to make sporting tours to South Africa was the right way to oppose apartheid, agreeing to make them in order to challenge vigorously the idea of the superiority of the Afrikaner was, arguably, the least wrong way. In which case, the 1974 Lions, spurred by McBride's captaincy, earned their redemption by winning twenty-one out of twenty-two matches and drawing the other. Alun Thomas, the tour manager, described McBride as an exceptional man. He said that the captain was 'literally worshipped by his players . . . because they saw in him all the things they would like to be'. Not all of McBride's ideas met the highest standards of sportsmanship, most notably his '99' call, which was a signal for all fifteen Lions players to physically assault the opposition. The justification was that previous teams had been cowed by Springbok aggression and a rallying cry would ensure not only a response but a concerted one. The third Test in Port Elizabeth, which the Lions won 26–9, was recalled by some veteran observers as the most violent international they could remember with McBride making the incendiary '99' call once in each half. If it had its desired effect of helping to win the series in South Africa, it was also believed to lie behind an increase in thuggish play in Britain. McBride was twenty-one when he made his debut in the second row for Ireland against England at Twickenham in 1962. He showed huge promise straightaway and was selected for the Lions tour of South Africa later that year. With natural strength that had been honed on the family farm, he was one of the few players from the British Isles who, in the 1960s and 1970s, had the physical presence and inner fibre to match the forwards from the southern hemisphere. Having seen up close the effect that bullying tactics had on British teams, McBride understood better than anyone that when he went on his fifth Lions tour in 1974, this time as captain, his team had to confront attempts to intimidate them. In his last appearance for Ireland at Lansdowne Road in 1975, McBride scored his first try in an international.

MARY RAND
⟞ 1940– ⟝

MARY RAND fitted her Golden Girl sobriquet as consummately as she did the mini-skirt and fur-collared suede jacket she wore to collect her MBE from the Queen in 1965. The winner of gold, silver and bronze medals at the 1964 Olympics in Tokyo, Rand paraded her athletic prowess and glamour with equal confidence. Even a young Mick Jagger took notice, nominating her as his 'dream date' in a teenage pop magazine. She was also an inspirational presence. Her long-jump victory in Tokyo put the spring in the step of her room-mate Ann Packer, who won the 800 metres six days later, and her example was what convinced Mary Peters she could win the pentathlon at the 1972 Olympics. Rand, born Mary Bignal, was brought up as one of nine in a council house in Somerset. She matured quickly as an athlete and at twenty was favourite to win the long jump at the 1960 Olympics in Rome. She led the qualifying competition but flopped in the final, fouling in two of her three jumps and finishing ninth. Perhaps the answer lay in her admission of having had extra-curricular fun: 'We were young, we were single, we were in Rome,' she said later. By 1964, she was married to the British Olympic oarsman Sidney Rand and had a daughter. This time she performed imperiously. The worst of her six efforts in the long jump final would have been enough to secure the silver medal; the best, on a soggy, cinder surface into a stiff headwind, set a world record of 6.76 metres (22 feet 2¼ inches). It made her the first British female to win an Olympic athletics gold. 'It was my day of days,' she said. She would have won a second gold medal had it not been for the presence of the Soviet athlete Irina Press, who disappeared from competition when sex tests were introduced before the 1966 European championships. Press's monster effort in the shot putt gave her a lead in the pentathlon that left Rand in second place. She completed her set of medals in Tokyo with a bronze when she ran the second leg in the sprint relay. Rand's range of events was such that she set British records for the long jump (eleven times), pentathlon, 100 yards, and 80 metres hurdles, in which she was fourth at the 1960 Olympics. She also held the national high jump title. She retired after injury prevented her competing at the 1968 Olympics. Although she was widely known as Mary Rand, the surname was that of the first of her three husbands.

ALEX FERGUSON
1941–

ALEX FERGUSON's implacable approach to management gave bulk and substance to the Manchester United blockbuster when it looked in danger of being reduced to a B-movie. The narrative lost its hero and its way when George Best opened the vodka bottle and released the genie that watched over his brilliance, but the cold shock of Ferguson's pragmatism finally rescued the plot. Ferguson was born in Govan in Glasgow, where you toiled in the Clyde shipyards, played football or got into trouble. Ferguson did the first two, becoming a staunch union man – 'Mammy thinks you're a bloody communist,' his grandmother once told him, confrontationally – and then a moderately successful forward at six Scottish clubs between 1958 and 1974. As a manager, his reputation for strict discipline was formed at Aberdeen, where on one occasion he fined a player for overtaking him on a public road. His firm control also brought results. In six seasons, Aberdeen won three championships, four Scottish Cups and the European Cup Winners' Cup, achievements that put the plutocrats of England on his case. In 1986, having overseen Scotland's effort at the World Cup finals in Mexico, Ferguson moved to Old Trafford. After a low point in what he called the 'Black December of 1989', when fans waved a banner that read, 'Three years of excuses: Ta-ra Fergie', the 1990 FA Cup success marked the start of the revival. Over the next decade Manchester United's consistency made them masters of the domestic game. In 1999, at the end of a season in which they won the Premiership title and FA Cup, they also claimed the European Cup with a 2–1 win over Bayern Munich, both United goals being scored in injury time. 'Football, bloody hell,' quipped Ferguson, who now received the recognition of a knighthood. Ferguson's tough leadership was a recurring theme in the club's renaissance. His dressing-room outbursts were so heated their effect was likened to that of a hair dryer, while one of their star turns, David Beckham, received a cut eye from a flying boot. On match days, Ferguson could be a fearsome figure on the touchline, standing wintry-faced and chewing gum relentlessly. His success was helped by a generation of outstanding players reared by the club, including Beckham and Paul Scholes, while his growing reputation for achieving results proved a powerful magnet for stars such as Eric Cantona,

Wayne Rooney and Ronaldo. When he entered his third decade in charge, he stood on a pedestal as elevated as any an English club manager has occupied and could reflect on a stewardship that had turned United in to the world's wealthiest club. United's ninth Premiership title under Ferguson in 2007 ended speculation that his appetite for success had grown jaded.

BOBBY MOORE
1941–1993

BOBBY MOORE was the antithesis of the defenders he would have watched play parks football when growing up on the fringes of London's East End. As a boy, he was never quite big enough to be apprenticed into the popular school of elemental defending and was fortunate, when he joined West Ham, to enrol into one of the few local establishments that encouraged sophistication. Whether it was a hard match or hard night-out, his poise never slipped (and, in the days before news desks turned their sanctimony on sybaritic footballers, there were plenty of the latter). On the pitch, his movement was unhurried and unfussed, yet he would dispossess opponents no matter how skilful, obdurate or fast. Having won the ball, he could then deliver a telling pass. 'There should be a law against him,' the Scotland manager Jock Stein said. 'He knows what's happening twenty minutes before anyone else.' The few seconds that best represented the essential Moore came at the end of the 1966 World Cup final. The England captain gained possession and disregarded the screamed entreaties of his team-mates and the Wembley crowd to hoof the ball into the stands. Instead he struck a long pass to Geoff

Hurst and England's 3–2 lead became 4–2. If that moment defined Moore, two images made him an indelible part of that era of rising national confidence of which The Beatles were also a part: the first, his chariot ride on the shoulders of England team members after the World Cup win over West Germany; the second, his embrace with Brazil's Pele at the 1970 World Cup, undiminished even in defeat. Moore gave his finest international performance in that match against Brazil, which took place only a few weeks after an incident that some thought was designed to subvert Moore's position as England captain. While the team were in Colombia for a warm-up match, Moore was accused of stealing a bracelet from a jewellery shop. It was some days, including four when he was held under house arrest, before he was released, illogically to play some of his best football. Moore was an unexceptional schoolboy footballer. He progressed through application and his willingness to listen. Happily, some of football's keenest thinkers happened to be at West Ham in the late 1950s and early 1960s: men such as Malcolm Allison and Ron Greenwood. This diligent approach brought him on quickly and he was only twenty-one when the England manager Walter Winterbottom included him in the squad that went to Chile for the 1962 World Cup. The following year he captained England for the first time and in 1964 he was given the job permanently by Alf Ramsey. 'My captain, my leader, my right-hand man. He was the spirit and the heartbeat of the team,' Ramsey said. 'Without him England would never have won the World Cup.' Moore spent his last three seasons playing for Fulham and then turned, unsuccessfully, to management at Southend and Oxford. He died of cancer before receiving the recognition, which was his due, of a knighthood.

MIKE BREARLEY

1942–

MIKE BREARLEY was a scholar and a cricketer – in that order, which makes it all the more remarkable that he achieved so much in what might be termed the lesser of his two fields. His intellect defined him in his professional lives as a cricketer and, later, an eminent psychoanalyst. In his student days, Brearley's sporting and academic accomplishments were equally impressive. At Cambridge, where his existence was a triptych of work, sleep and play, he took a first in Classics and a 2:1 in Moral Sciences while scoring 4,310 first-class runs in four seasons for the university, an aggregate that may never be surpassed. He made a triple century when captaining an MCC under-25 team in Pakistan in 1966–7, but the weight of runs became less crushing as his career matured at Middlesex and with England. What marked him out latterly was his captaincy, to which he brought tactical nous and man-management skills that comfortably compensated for his modest contributions as a batsman. He conducted himself without a hint of intellectual snobbery, and knew how to connect with his players. His techniques included the unsubtle remarks he used to gee up one of the finest of those who served under him, the all-rounder Ian Botham. One was, 'My aunt bowls faster than you'; and another, which Brearley said really got Botham going because it invoked a team-mate notoriously prone to mystical impediments, 'Chris Old has the edge over you today.' On the other hand, he could deliver sentences that were beyond the refinement of most sportsmen, as in: 'You have to try to reply to criticism with your intellect, not your ego.' He summed up the difficulties of cricket captaincy compared to other tasks involving responsibility by pointing out in his best-selling book *The Art of Captaincy*: 'Sales managers don't sell, foremen don't hump bricks. All cricket captains bat and field, and some bowl. We receive repeated intimations of our own fallibility.' He first led England in 1977, after the media revealed that the man he succeeded, Tony Greig, had been an accomplice of the Australian tycoon Kerry Packer in establishing the breakaway World Series Cricket. In 1980, Botham inherited the captaincy, but the experiment unravelled as quickly as Botham's form and the selectors issued what amounted to an SOS to Brearley midway through the 1981 home series against Australia. Brearley's mind and Botham's muscle wrestled back the initiative and the Ashes were dramatically retained. Brearley averaged only 22.88 as a Test batsman. The more telling statistic was the seven series England won of the nine in which Brearley captained them.

LYNN DAVIES
1942–

LYNN DAVIES competed in the long jump for the first time on his last sports day at Ogmore Grammar School in South Wales in 1961. The miner's son who had hoped to make it as a footballer or rugby player took off into what he said was not a proper long-jump pit, 'just a hole in the ground, which the council used to come and fill up with a ton of sand'. He jumped 21 feet 2½ inches, two feet beyond the qualifying standard for the Glamorgan schools championships that were to be held in two weeks' time. 'You could be quite good at this, Lynn,' said his startled games master. At the championships, he cleared more than 22 feet in front of Ron Pickering, the newly appointed national coach who would become his mentor. Barely three years later at the age of twenty-two, he would become Wales's first Olympic champion. On a foul October night in Tokyo, he won the title at the 1964 Games by beating the American world-record holder, Ralph Boston, and his great rival, the powerful Russian Igor Ter-Ovanesyan. After four rounds, no one had jumped close to eight metres and Davies overheard Boston say that he did not think the distance was possible in the conditions. This gave Davies the confidence that he could pull off a major upset because, not long before, he had jumped more than eight metres in the rain while training in Cardiff. As he prepared for his fifth jump, he noticed from a flag on top of the stadium that the wind had dropped. The flag remained limp during Davies's run-up, he hit the take-off board perfectly and sailed out to 8.07 metres (26 feet 5¾ inches). Boston rallied to clear eight metres himself but finished three centimetres behind Davies, whose jump earned him the abiding nickname 'Lynn the Leap'. It would be Britain's last Olympic field-event title by a male athlete for thirty-six years, a barren spell ended only when Jonathan Edwards won the triple jump at the Sydney Games in 2000. In 1968, Davies, who was also one of Britain's top three sprinters, extended the British record to 8.23 metres, which survived until broken by Chris Tomlinson in 2002. A PE teacher when he won his Olympic title, Davies stayed fit and trim into later life and taught at the University of Wales Institute Cardiff, where he was senior lecturer in the school of sport and physical education.

TONY JACKLIN
1944–

TONY JACKLIN was a fierce wind of change in golf whipped up as if from nowhere. He stirred a long, benign spell in the European game when he arrived on the scene accompanied by a precocious talent and grating cockiness. The arrogance was almost certainly a response to his coming from outside the game's established milieu – he was a lorry driver's son from Scunthorpe – and did not last. In the 1980s he finished off the renaissance he had inspired in Europe by being an inspirational Ryder Cup captain. In 1968, he won the Jacksonville Open, the first victory on America's PGA tour by a UK player, to alert the golfing world to his potential – and of the possibility of winning on the other side of the Atlantic. His golden years were 1969 to 1972 when he gave the British game as big a boost as Arnold Palmer had the US's more than a decade before. He ended nearly two decades of Open championships without a British win by taking the 1969 title at Royal Lytham. In the autumn of that year at Royal Birkdale, he dragged Great Britain and Ireland to a wholly unexpected tie in the Ryder Cup, the 16–16 scoreline secured when Jack Nicklaus sportingly conceded a three-foot putt to give Jacklin a half. (In later life, as a slightly forlorn figure, Jacklin helped out at Nicklaus's club in Florida named The Concession after the American's gesture at Birkdale.) Although he referred to winning the 1969 Open as 'my Everest', in the estimation of most other people Jacklin went even higher a year later when he triumphed at Hazeltine, Minnesota, to become the first player since Ben Hogan to hold the US and British Open titles. He led from the start to win by seven shots, the largest margin in forty-nine years. 'I walked on water that week,' he said. The extraordinary fury with which he arrived would give way to a steep fall-off in results, his successes increasingly dominated by disappointments. He challenged strongly in the 1972 Open at Muirfield before finishing third and topped Europe's order of merit in 1973. By the early 1980s, he had had enough. 'Golf was the only thing I did that didn't make me happy so I stopped doing it,' he said. He rediscovered his passion for the game and a real talent for leadership when made captain of the Ryder Cup team in 1983. He bolstered the team's confidence, brought in cashmere for nylon and Concorde for BA economy, and they responded by losing only once in his four stints as captain. The successes included the first away win by Great Britain and Ireland or Europe, a 15–13 margin at Muirfield Village, Columbus, in 1987.

JIMMY JOHNSTONE
1944–2006

JIMMY JOHNSTONE was the incarnation of every schoolboy's notion of the ideal footballer, and the champion of every small man tired of the bigger man's assumed superiority. The prestidigitation 'Jinky' Johnstone performed with his feet drove plenty of big men mad enough to resort to physical retribution, which brought out Johnstone's other great quality:

physical courage. One obituarist wrote of Johnstone that, in view of how dirty football was in the 1960s, it was hardly surprising his 'fellow players were in awe of his courage even more than they were of his talent'. Billy McNeill, captain of the Celtic team who won the 1967 European Cup in Lisbon, said Johnstone was 'as sharp as a tack, as fit as anything, as brave as a lion'. Johnstone, once voted Celtic's greatest ever player, was emblematic of those 'Lisbon Lions' with his speed and artistry. He ultimately embarrassed Milan's Internazionale in a 2–1 victory that made the Glasgow team Britain's first European champions. Johnstone showed his determination to make it as a footballer, despite being only 5 feet 2 inches when he was sixteen, by slogging out training miles in his father's pit boots. He did put on height and weight, but he never escaped the attention of the bully boys, who in the shape of the Atlético Madrid team in the Glasgow leg of the 1974 European Cup semi-final tried their best to eliminate his potency in every sense of that phrase. Johnstone was involved in numerous scrapes, none more widely publicised than when in 1974 he was cast out to sea in a rowing boat, without oars, after the Scotland squad emerged from a pub in Ayrshire. 'I thought I'd go fishing,' said the drily humorous Johnstone after he was rescued by the coastguard some distance from shore. Four days later he answered his critics with a typically effervescent performance in a 2–0 win over England. Johnstone was sixty-one when he died of motor neuron disease, a particularly malign fate for a player whose command of movement had been so mesmerising. At the funeral mass, Joseph Devine, the Bishop of Motherwell, alluded to Johnstone's battle with drink and other distractions by saying that he made more use of the confessional box than any other Celtic player. The bishop also told of the exclamation of the elderly fan sitting next to him at a match: 'Father, please forgive the bad language, but see the wee man – is that not sheer bloody poetry.'

BARRY JOHN
1945–

BARRY JOHN was the rugby union fly-half in excelcis. In the pre-professional era this brought him no benefit other than adulation, which was why he retired early. He said he was particularly troubled by the hero-worship. 'I never sought adulation, that's probably why I ran away from it.' This mortified many thousands of Wales supporters – and disappointed many thousands more around the world who simply enjoyed watching someone who could so gracefully pick his way through ranks of powerful men wanting to maim him. Carmarthenshire Police were among the first to rumble John's huge promise, but had to give him an assumed name when he played for them because he was still a sixth former at Gwendraeth Grammar School. John told the story of being intercepted by a teacher who threatened to call the police when she caught him leaving school before lessons were over. He told her she could not do that – he was on his way to play rugby for them. With his immense talent, John could have made his international debut earlier than he did but the selectors delayed risking their prized new asset until December 1966, a month before his twenty-second birthday. He was an immediate success. Although Barry John was, above all, a name that resonated in Wales, its far wider echo swelled from the 1971 Lions tour of New Zealand. He had decided not to go on that tour having been injured putting in a try-saving tackle on the mighty Benoît Dauga of France in the Five Nations, but the Lions coach Carwyn James, who lived close to him in Cefneithin, talked him round. John's contribution to the Lions' first series win in New Zealand was a thing of wonder, his kicking, running and tactical acumen lifting the whole team to outperform a thoroughly worthy All Black side. It was on this tour that he became known as The King and the public adulation in Britain reached a pitch that helped persuade him to retire soon afterwards. He disliked it when Eamonn Andrews ambushed him to appear on *This Is Your Life* and there were several other incidents, one in particular. He was invited to open the extension of a bank and the crowd cheered and applauded wildly when a small girl curtsied to him. 'If I needed something to show me that it had all gone way over the top, that was it,' he said. As an amateur, he was also conscious that getting out of the game with his celebrity at its peak made commercial sense. So, at the age of twenty-seven, King Barry, having played only twenty-five times for his country, walked away to write a newspaper column and exploit his fame.

GEORGE BEST
━━ 1946–2005 ━━

GEORGE BEST started by making fools of his local football club, Glentoran, who thought him too fragile for his own genius – and went on to make fools of just about every defender he played against. Manchester United's reward for having faith in him was a player who in the estimation of millions, some of them even from outside Northern Ireland, stood comparison with Pelé and Maradona, despite his never having the opportunity to showcase himself at a World Cup. The Greek tragedy that would overtake him did nothing to reduce his distinction as a footballer. Best was born on the Cregagh Estate in Belfast, an area that despite its deprivations exercises a strong pull on those who leave. It nearly lured the fifteen-year-old Best back before he overcame homesickness. He made his Manchester United debut at seventeen and from 1963 to 1973 was the most exciting sight in British football. A natty dresser off the pitch, Best had something of the street urchin about him when he played: shirt outside his shorts, socks always threatening to tumble down, hands clutching at his cuffs and arms held awkwardly away from his body. The class was in his movement, those arms positioned to provide balance while his feet – his left as effective as his right – exercised an uncanny control over the ball. He made even good defenders look inept, and he would occasionally go back and make them look inept again. There was nothing he did on a football pitch that he did not do well, but the enduring memory was his goal scoring, for United and in 37 appearances for Northern Ireland. The brilliant goal when he deceived and then rounded the keeper in United's 4–1 win over Benfica in the 1968 European Cup final was no more than typical of so many others he scored. Alcohol destroyed his career and then him. He left

Manchester United when still only twenty-seven and the rest of his playing career was mostly a sorry exercise in clubs signing him in the vain hope he might be persuaded to reverse the irreversible consequences of his addiction. Not enough people told him he was an objectionable drunk, and those who did were ignored. He died after his transplanted liver, which he abused as wilfully as the original, failed. The drawn-out process of his death was attended by the relentless publicity that had helped to destabilise his life.

ALAN KNOTT
1946–

ALAN KNOTT came out of the wicketkeeping garden of England. He was probably the most brilliant, and undeniably the most idiosyncratic, of a line of outstanding Kent glovemen that included his England predecessors Leslie Ames and Godfrey Evans. He was a friendly but self-contained man who was fastidious in all things, most notably in matters of health and hygiene when preparing for and playing cricket. He made sure of his eight hours' sleep each night and, with his devotion to exercise, needed two more hours to prepare for the day. He was small and nimble with a distinctive profile, the jutting chin giving him a look of Mr Punch. His method when standing up to the stumps, developed at Kent while keeping to the guileful Derek Underwood on rain-affected pitches, included taking the low ball without flexing his knees and with legs together to provide an extra barrier against byes. He was acrobatic when standing back, overly so in the judgement of some, but he argued that his success rate – a missed chance by Knott was a collector's item – justified the occasional extravagance. As a number-seven batsman who passed 50 in 30 of his 149 Test innings, he was, according to one of his England captains, Mike Brearley, a minor genius, with a technique that was all of a one with his quirky personality. He turned his head straight at the bowler, fixed him with a wide-eyed stare and ducked low as he raised his bat, which he held away from his body in an open stance. He fiddled with his grip to suit the type of bowler. Against the quickest he shifted his top hand behind the handle to keep the blade straight when defending. He loved to sweep slower bowlers, once doing so 15 balls in a row against Middlesex's England spinners John Emburey and Phil Edmonds – each time connecting with the meat of the bat. Born in Kent, he played for the county for twenty-one years and in 95 Tests from 1967 to 1981. When he retired from the first-class game approaching his fortieth birthday, he was still keeping wicket so well he was close to an England recall. He was criticised for joining the rebel tour of South Africa in 1982. His logic for doing so was as individual as his cricket: 'Being a Christian, I cannot imagine a missionary saying, "We won't go there until apartheid is finished".'

GARETH EDWARDS
1947–

GARETH EDWARDS was the strong, unstillable heartbeat of the great Wales rugby union sides of the 1970s. In the Decade of the Dragon – 1969 to 1979 – Wales won the Five Nations eight times and were never out of the top two. His contribution stood out even in a team who were an extraordinary coalition of talent. A miner's son from Gwaun-cae-Gurwen, Edwards went to Millfield, a public school that offered sports scholarships to children from families of limited means. He was an outstanding athlete and gymnast who was ideally suited to the pivotal position of scrum-half with the upper body of a welterweight boxer and explosive speed. He delivered a monstrously long pass, having practised with a ball filled with sand. While still a nineteen-year-old student at the Cardiff College of Education, he started a run of fifty-three consecutive appearances for Wales. A year later he was made Wales's youngest captain at twenty years and seven months. In 1969, Wales swamped England 30–9 in Cardiff to reclaim the Five Nations title and, although they did not know it yet, the other four nations were now in their thrall, effectively for the next ten years. In addition to his contributions for Wales, Edwards was a mighty presence for the Lions, including in series victories against New Zealand and South Africa. For thousands, though, the side for which Edwards made his most memorable appearance was the Barbarians in the 23–11 win over the All Blacks at Cardiff in 1973. Edwards's flamboyant dive completed the move, launched close to the Barbarians' posts by his half-back partner Phil Bennett and carried on almost exclusively by Wales players, that became known simply as The Try. In an all-round celebration of Welsh creativity, it was embellished by Cliff Morgan's commentary for BBC Television, a masterpiece of composed breathlessness. The humorist and rugby fan Spike Milligan also had his say. Milligan's wit could be biting, but on this occasion he was moved to be elegiac: 'Edwards was a poet that day, not a rugby player. He was a ballet dancer, a pugilist, a mathematician.' Edwards himself was a humorous man, on the pitch as well as off it. During a Lions Test in South Africa, he nearly had the life squeezed from him when a pile of players pinned him to the sun-baked surface. When they peeled away, they left Edwards looking up at the first-aid attendants who had rushed to his side. 'Don't move me, bury me,' he said. His one-liners also helped to establish the popularity of the BBC Television programme *A Question of Sport*.

ALEX HIGGINS
1949–

ALEX HIGGINS provided lurid proof of how an addictive gene can subvert virtuous ones. Higgins's dependency on alcohol and nicotine, a need on public display whenever he played snooker, fuelled an ugly paranoia that sabotaged his staggering ability. Between his two world titles in 1972 and 1982, Higgins, known as 'Hurricane', played thrilling, high-speed, edgy snooker whose excitement so permeated the game that through his efforts alone it became a television favourite. He was a compelling spectacle as he prowled around a table, face and cue twitching, until he somehow calmed himself just long enough to dispatch the ball with laser accuracy. In time, though, his excesses upset what was always a finely calibrated psyche with unpleasant consequences for both his behaviour and his snooker. Born in Belfast, Higgins learnt to play in the city's Jampot club. At one time he trained to be a jockey but his success in amateur snooker events persuaded him this was his future and he turned professional in 1971. He claimed the world championship at his first attempt in 1972, when the prize money was £480, by beating John Spencer 37–32 in the final. Spencer was a member of the old, clean-cut school and his defeat by Higgins marked snooker's passing into more febrile times. Players such as Jimmy White and Ronnie O'Sullivan followed him down the path of agitating the steady rhythms and rigid etiquette of the professional game's early years. Higgins lost in two world finals, 1976 and 1980, before winning the title again in 1982 with a 135 clearance that clinched his 18–15 win over Ray Reardon. The 69 break in the penultimate frame of his semi-final against White that year was regarded as one of the finest passages of play ever seen. From 0–59 behind, and one ball away from elimination, he cleared the table despite being out of position for nearly every shot until he came to the colours. Despite this there were already signs that he was losing control over his game and his personal conduct. His decline turned nasty in 1986 when he butted an official in a dispute that started when he was asked to give a urine sample. Disintegration followed as every attempt at rehabilitation ended in tears and preposterous outbursts, such as threatening to have his fellow Northern Irishman Dennis Taylor shot. One of the few bright spots in his later years was a successful operation for throat cancer. Otherwise he cut an increasingly pathetic figure with the millions of pounds he was once worth long gone and stories circulating of how he would play for relatively small sidestakes in pubs and clubs. Only the distant luminosity of a capacity for playing snooker superbly well was left.

J. P. R. WILLIAMS
— 1949– —

J. P. R. WILLIAMS stirred fearlessness, competitive vigour and athleticism into a mix that made him rugby union's sovereign full back – but he might have become a professional tennis player. In 1966 he beat David Lloyd, who went on to appear in a Davis Cup final, to win the junior championship of Great Britain before, two years later, he collected £20 after qualifying for the first open tournament in tennis history. He drove straight from that tournament in Bournemouth to Bridgend, where his performance in a big win over Newport convinced the Wales rugby selectors to pick him. He would be around for more than a decade of Five Nations matches, forty-five in all, of which only seven were lost – none of them against England. His immense contributions to the Lions' winning tours to Australasia in 1971 and South Africa in 1974 reinforced his reputation. As the son of two doctors, Williams came from outside the social circle of most of his colleagues of the great Wales sides of the 1970s. He said this was an extra motivating factor. Being middle-class, he said, made him much more determined to prove himself, which was why he developed into such a brave player. This bravery included staying on the field at all costs, even, for 25 minutes, with a fractured cheekbone in a match against Scotland. Williams's competitive drive was such that on the 1971 Lions tour he was banned from some of the training sessions because he was injuring too many of his team-mates with his fierce tackling. He derived such a buzz from playing for Wales in Cardiff that when he looked in the mirror his 'eyeballs would be up and I'd have to tell myself "Calm down"'. With his long hair, rolled-down socks and high-stepping running style, Williams was an unmistakable figure. If he was not defending his line with the ferocity of an enraged beast, he was looking for opportunities to break down field with buccaneering charges. It was said that kicking was not his strongest point, a criticism that was heard less often after his drop goal from 50 yards helped the 1971 Lions draw the final Test against the All Blacks and win the series. 'The ball was still climbing as it went through the posts,' he said. 'I hit it perfectly.' Inevitably, given the robust nature of his game, he attracted offers from rugby league, including £10,000 plus trimmings to sign for Hull. Instead, having inflicted so many wounds, Williams spent the rest of his life mending them as an orthopaedic surgeon.

BARRY SHEENE
1950–2003

BARRY SHEENE lived out the dream of every underachieving schoolboy turned motorcycle messenger by becoming a world champion on a 500 cc Suzuki. With likely-lad good looks, he also realised that other part of the dream as a magnet for women who fancied men zipped up to the throat in leathers. Brought up in central London, where his father worked as resident engineer for the Royal College of Surgeons, Sheene was the British 125 cc champion by the time he was twenty and in 1971 he finished second in the world championship for that class. Even though he was a clever racer, who was happy to leave the desperado stuff to others, he could not escape the sport's inherent danger when a rear tyre blew while he was touching 175 mph at the Daytona 200 in Florida in 1975. He suffered internal injuries, broke his right arm, collarbone and two ribs and needed to have an 18-inch pin inserted in his left thigh to hold it together. He amazed doctors with his recovery, which saw him racing again less than two months later. The next year he won the 500 cc world championship, to give the Suzuki factory team their first victory; he retained the title in 1977 and was runner-up in 1978. These three years were to be the high noon of his racing career. He grew unsettled at Suzuki, where he thought he was receiving inferior equipment, and after the 1979 season went freelance on a Yamaha, although the manufacturers soon moved in to support him. His second major accident, this time during practice for the British Grand Prix at Silverstone in 1982, effectively ended his career as a rider. He was in the operating theatre for seven hours as surgeons pieced his shattered legs back together. Although he raced again, he retired in 1984 when he accepted he was no longer a title contender. A serious and excellent racer, Sheene was gregarious and likeable away from the track; he was smart enough to realise the advantage of cultivating his image as a chirpy Cockney

geezer. It helped him secure sponsorship and endorsement deals that financed the standard trappings of wealth, a Rolls-Royce parked on the gravel drive outside his manor house. In the late 1980s, he moved to Australia, hoping the sunshine would alleviate the pain he still felt in his patched-up limbs. At one time he had 28 screws in his legs (and a bolt in his left wrist). He remained in demand for television work, finding renewed popularity as a commentator with a nudge-nudge line in patter, and he also enjoyed racing historic motorcycles. He died of cancer.

JOCKY WILSON
1950–

JOCKY WILSON brought the hope of sporting glory to small, portly men before his life went into a drink-induced decline. 'I'm short and fat, so what? That's life,' he said. 'Anyway, TV makes you look fatter.' The reference to television was recognition of the medium that made Wilson one of the best known faces and bellies in Britain in the 1980s when he twice won the world darts title. This was before satellite brodcasting when darts events – as many as eleven were screened annually – attracted audiences of more than eight million. This exposure, coupled with the sport's simplicity and accessibility in pubs and clubs, put darts' popularity on an upward curve throughout the decade. Remarkably, considering Wilson's huge alcohol intake – lager chased by 'seven or eight vodkas to keep my nerves so that I can play my best' – he remained sufficiently millimetre-accurate to reach at least the quarter-finals of the world championships every year between 1979 and 1991. The effect of his drinking was evident after a world semi-final in 1984, in which Wilson lost 5–4 to Dave Whitcombe after being in control of the match. When the BBC cameraman swung back to where the Scot had been standing, there was no sign of him – because he had fallen off the stage. Wilson, born in Kirkcaldy, Scotland, worked in the coal industry as a delivery man and miner. The chance to make something of his precise darts throwing came during a period of unemployment in 1979 when he won a competition at Butlins that earned him a prize of £500. Later that

BEST OF BRITISH

JOCKY WILSON

year he entered his first world championship and made it to the last eight. He reached the quarter-finals in each of the next two years before in 1982 he won through to the final where he beat John Lowe 5–3. His second world title in 1989 came after a thrilling match in which he defeated his great rival Eric Bristow 6–4 having led 5–0. He was a quarter-finalist twice more before his drinking started to affect his play and he suffered first-round defeats in 1992 and 1993. He never announced his retirement, but by the mid-1990s it was clear his career was over as health and financial problems – he was declared bankrupt in 1997 – bore down on his morale. 'I'm all washed up and finished with darts,' he said. Afflicted by depression, diabetes and arthritis, Wilson withdrew to the backroom of a council flat in Kirkcaldy. His wife, Malvina, the cheerful keeper of his front door, said: 'It's just the bed and TV for him now.'

KENNY DALGLISH
1951–

KENNY DALGLISH rejected the sort of flamboyance, on and off the pitch, that many in football would have regarded as obligatory had they achieved much less than he did. Instead, he looked out at the world from behind a deadpan stare that particularly frustrated goalkeepers and journalists. He once crossed the street to inform a reporter: 'Wisnae.' And that was it. It transpired Dalglish was telling him he was wrong to have written he was off-side, because he 'wisnae'; this, the journalist observed, was more information than Dalglish had ever previously given him. He communicated all that he wanted through his results as a scorer and maker of goals and then as a player-manager and manager. He won fourteen league championships with Celtic, Liverpool and Blackburn in his various capacities, helped Liverpool to three European Cups and was the first player to appear 100 times for Scotland, finishing with 102 caps. His sombre exterior proved sadly appropriate when his life was touched by three of football's blackest episodes: the 1971 Ibrox disaster in which 66 people died when Stairway 13 collapsed; the riot at the 1985 Liverpool v Juventus European Cup final at Heysel that resulted in 39 deaths; and the 1989 Hillsborough tragedy when 96 spectators at the Liverpool end lost their lives at an FA Cup semi-final. Dalglish was present at all three and, while he was rightly praised for his caring response to Hillsborough, the effect on him of that dire event contributed to his resignation as Liverpool manager in 1991. Dalglish was brought up near the Govan docklands in Glasgow and supported Rangers, which meant bedroom posters had to be hurriedly torn down when Celtic came knocking. His first goal for Celtic was against Rangers during a League Cup win in 1971–2. A penalty, it was unrepresentative of the goal-scoring for which he became renowned. For Dalglish, scoring was more a craft than a photo opportunity and his craftsmanship was constantly on display. He was the first player to score 100 goals in the Scottish and English leagues and he equalled Denis Law's record of 30 goals for Scotland. When Ian Rush joined him at Liverpool, he took as much pleasure from creating goals for Wales's master marksman as he did from scoring them. He became almost impossible to dispossess as he refined the art of shielding the ball and knew precisely when to release it into Rush's path. Despite winning a Premiership title with Blackburn in 1995 to join the small band of managers to have guided two clubs to the title, Dalglish's career after leaving Liverpool was disappointing. Post Anfield, he never quite brought the same wild-eyed intensity to his work.

NIGEL MANSELL
1953–

NIGEL MANSELL gained acceptance as a motor racer less ordinary when the public finally warmed to the mix of anti-heroic persona off the track and pugnacious excellence on it. An expression whose blandness could look cultivated and a voice that sounded like an electric tool running low on power also made it an effort to like him. In the end, though, even the sniping remarks about him – 'He's an uneducated blockhead' (fellow driver Nelson Piquet), 'He'll never win a grand prix as long as I've got a hole in my arse' (team manager Peter Warr) and 'In a car he's magic, but out of it he's a pain in the back-side' (team boss Frank Williams) – somehow merged into a

147

collective backslap. Mansell, born in Upton-on-Severn, Worcestershire, used his own money to get started in motor racing. He developed his crash-and-burn approach in karting before moving through Formula Ford and Formula Three. As British world champions Jim Clark and Graham Hill had done before him, Mansell then joined Formula One in 1980 after impressing the Lotus boss Colin Chapman. After five years Mansell left Lotus for Williams, where he spent most of the rest of his career. He had two seasons at Ferrari (1989–90) after being the last driver personally selected by Enzo Ferrari before his death in 1988. For Mansell, it was always a question of win or bust – the official count was 31 grand prix wins, more than any other Brit, and 32 crashes – a fact that endeared him to the Italian *tifosi* who called him Il Leone in his Ferrari-driving days. It was the same out of the car, with Mansell enjoying strong friendships alongside the smouldering wrecks of others. Alain Prost, for one, became a despised adversary. There were numerous threats to retire before he finally did in 1994 after 187 hard-driven races. He was forty-one. Mansell eventually won the Formula One world title in a Williams in 1992, dominating the championship with 14 pole positions and 9 wins in 16 races. The next year he went off to the US where he showed just what a versatile driver he was by winning the CART title. It was the first instance of a driver holding both these premier titles at the same time. The two defining images of Mansell were the scary rear-tyre blow-out at the 1986 Australian Grand Prix that deprived him of the world title, and almost cost him his life, and the scene of fans mobbing him after he rolled to a halt having won the 1992 British Grand Prix. They encapsulated his life on the edge and his relationship to a public who conceded in the end that they had to love him.

IAN BOTHAM
1955–

IAN BOTHAM was, above all, a combative cricketer who ridiculed the idea that high achievement was the preserve of craftsmen. He batted and bowled with a robustness and relish that made light of, but did not wholly ignore, the small print of technical correctness. He could empty bars quicker than a fire alarm, never more so than in 1985 when his 80 sixes in a season eclipsed the record of Somerset's other cherished hitter, Arthur Wellard. He was an equally committed, if considerably less successful, footballer whose performances in defence for Scunthorpe defined the word clogger. Born in Cheshire, Botham arrived at Somerset in 1973 and flourished in a dressing room populated by strong characters such as the pugnacious former England captain Brian Close. He would, though, break with Somerset thirteen years later after an acrimonious dispute over the county's decision to release his great friends Viv Richards and Joel Garner. By 1977, Botham's striking all-round performances at Taunton – punitive batting and competitive swing bowling – earned him an England call-up for the third Test against Australia at Trent Bridge. He banished fears that he had been brought into the side with ill-judged haste by taking 5 for 74, 4 of the wickets coming in a 34-ball spell. He contributed only 25 with the bat but it was England's third highest score and his international career had been successfully launched. It lasted until 1992, by which time he had played in 102 Tests and 116 one-day internationals, and included an annus mirabilis in 1981 that featured a memorable Ashes Test at Headingley. England lost their seventh second-innings wicket at 135, still 92 behind Australia's first innings total, before Botham's 149 not out, with his hundred coming off 87 balls, transformed a match that England won by 18 runs. In the Edgbaston Test that followed, Botham took 5 wickets for 1 run in 28 balls in a 29-run victory. That summer alone assured Botham would be forgiven his unsuccessful stint as England captain, his failure to make an impression on the dominant West Indians and an unexemplary private life that became as reported on as his public one. A media campaign led to his being banned for taking cannabis in 1986, but he bounced back with typical brio. Recalled against New Zealand at the Oval, he dismissed batsmen with his second and twelfth balls to equal and pass Dennis Lillee's then-world record of 355 Test wickets. Later on, he amazed in even unlikelier ways. The pot-puffing roisterer was chosen by a breakfast-cereal manufacturer as the wholesome figurehead of an advertising campaign. Less surprisingly, he made a second career as a TV analyst purveying trenchant, quickfire views. He was an indefatigable fundraiser for charity, undertaking walks of hundreds of miles that he conducted at a brisk pace. An ardent monarchist, who once walked out of a dinner in Australia when the entertainer defamed the Queen, Botham received the highest notification that his several indiscretions were forgiven when he was knighted in 2007.

KELLY HOLMES

PART EIGHT

GILDED GENERATION
1955–1979

STEVE OVETT

1955–

STEVE OVETT was an extravagantly gifted athlete with an edgy personality, a mix that produced a supreme racer in the golden era of British middle-distance running. Born in Brighton, the son of a market trader, he was the archetypal long-haired art student of the 1970s. He could be cussed or charming, gracious or graceless, awkward or accommodating. He reserved constancy for when he was running, which he did as naturally and effortlessly as most people walk. The wave before the finish when he won was interpreted by some as arrogance, by others as an understandable expression of joy at being so good. The performances that first made him widely known were his 800 metres victory as a seventeen-year-old at the 1973 European junior championships and the silver medal over the same distance at the full European championships in Rome a year later. It was hoped that he might manage something at the 1976 Olympics in Montreal, but the monster stride of Cuba's Alberto Juantorena dominated the two-lap final, in which Ovett came a demoralised fifth. By 1980, Ovett was at the height of his capabilities. His meetings with team-mate Sebastian Coe at the Moscow Olympics were as compelling as track racing can be. In 1979, Coe had lowered Juantorena's record for the 800 metres by a full second. Ovett, cast as the baddy to the personable Coe's goody, was expected to chase Coe home in the shorter race and win the 1500 metres, which by now was his better distance. In a tactical 800 metres final, which suited Ovett, the drama unfolded in the last quarter. Ovett elbowed his way out of trouble, burst past the Russian Nikolai Kirov and had stretched too far ahead before Coe

BEST OF BRITISH

STEVE OVETT

responded. Ovett's time was more than three seconds slower than Coe's world record. Ovett, who said he was 90 per cent sure he would also win the 1500, looked as good as his prediction until Coe's desolation at losing a week earlier spurred him to the front. In the end, Ovett managed only third. Ovett competed for another ten years, running fast times – including five world records – and wonderful races, but his rivalry with Coe in Moscow was what best defined him. The effects of bronchitis overcame him at the 1984 Olympics in Los Angeles. He finished last in the 800 final and failed to complete the 1500. His last exit from the Olympics was on a stretcher. In middle age, Ovett lost most of his hair and the angst that once ignited his competitive fires. He went with his wife and four children to live in Australia.

SEBASTIAN COE
— 1956– —

SEBASTIAN COE was as clinically effective a middle-distance runner as he was aesthetically pleasing to watch. Beautifully balanced and with a long, light step, he also possessed a super-efficient cardiovascular system. From these, he and his father, Peter, who coached him obsessively throughout his running career, extracted everything that was available. Even when Coe was only seventeen, his father was predicting his son would break world records by significant amounts. In 1979, he broke three in forty-one days – 800 metres, a mile and 1500 metres. Britain's depth of athletic talent meant that at the 1980 Olympics in Moscow Coe and his team-mate Steve Ovett were the leading contenders for the 800 and 1500 metres. Their rivalry was sharpened by the media who played up the contrast between Coe's social skills and

BEST OF BRITISH

SEBASTIAN COE

Ovett's gaucheness. When Coe lost to Ovett in the 800-metres final, he faced the prospect of a heartbreaking double defeat with the 1500 metres regarded, at this stage, as his weaker event. He responded with a supremely competitive run, chasing down the East German Jürgen Straub to leave Ovett in third place. Four years later in Los Angeles, Coe became the first person to retain the Olympic 1500 metres title and took silver again in the 800 metres. After setting four world records in 1981, in the 800, the 1,000 and twice in the mile, he had been struck down by a condition eventually diagnosed as toxoplasmosis, a rare and debilitating infection. He did not resume training until December 1983, by which time another British runner, Steve Cram, had emerged as his main challenger over 1500 metres. In the Olympic final, it was Cram who pushed Coe to an Olympic-record 3 minutes 32.53 seconds. As he crossed the line, the normally restrained Coe gave a rare glimpse of the inner man when he turned to roar 'Who says I am finished?' at the British press, who had dismissed his chances. Coe once again battled illness to be fit for a second defence of his Olympic title in Seoul in 1988 and was aggrieved not to be picked. He set twelve world records and his time of 1 minute 41.73 seconds for the 800 metres stood for sixteen years. Coe's impressive results over a number of years, many in the face of medical problems, attracted some sceptical comment about how he had managed it, but nothing was proved and his reputation as an athlete survived without tarnish. Later he entered politics as a Conservative MP. When he failed to get re-elected he launched a second sporting career as judo instructor to the new leader of the Tory party, William Hague – although, officially, he was Hague's chief of staff. He received a peerage in 2002. In 2005, his leadership secured London's bid to stage the 2012 Olympics.

NICK FALDO
ᐧ——ᐧ 1957– ᐧ——ᐧ

NICK FALDO sacrificed the pursuit of perfection in other areas of his life to stalk it with an unbending will on the golf course. Three broken marriages were evidence of sacrifices in his private life; the ninety-eight weeks he spent as the world's number one and the six major titles the proof of a very commendable stab at flawlessness in his professional existence. An only child brought up in a small council house in Welwyn Garden City, Faldo applied an unusual amount of dedication to turning himself into a champion golfer – and then applied some more once he had reached a standard that would have satisfied most players. He was prepared to forgo nearly two years of his competitive career in the mid-1980s to mould a swing that was pressure-proof. The dividend was impressive although, being Faldo, he felt it could have been more. Faldo started playing golf manically after watching Jack Nicklaus competing in the Masters on television. He turned professional in 1976 and in 1983 finished top of Europe's order of merit. But the inconsistency that delighted headline writers, who dubbed him 'Nick Foldo', prompted the drastic stripping down and reassembling of his swing. In 1987 he won his first Open title at Muirfield and between then and the summer of 1992, during which time he won two more Opens and two Masters, he gained the same level of mastery over his rivals as Arnold Palmer and Nicklaus once did. He had one more memorable day in the Georgia sunshine when in 1996 he won his third Masters. He produced a performance of such grim steadiness that the Australian Greg Norman surrendered the six-stroke lead he held after three rounds. The American player Mark Calcavecchia gave a glimpse of how lonely Norman must have felt that day: 'When he's out playing Faldo doesn't say [anything]. Playing with Nick Faldo is like playing by yourself – only slower.' His individual successes in the US were key to convincing Europe's Ryder Cup players that the trophy did not necessarily have to be won by the side with American accents. In return, the competition brought out the team player in Faldo that few thought existed and in semi-retirement he would be named as Europe's captain for 2008. He played in eleven Ryder Cups and took part in a record forty-six matches, winning twenty-three of them. It was not only the women in his life he fell out of love with, in the case of the jilted Valerie Bercher with explosive repercussions when she trashed his Porsche with a golf club. Relationships with family, coaches, caddies and the media all went through hard times, too. After his third Open win at Muirfield in 1992, he publicly thanked his 'close friends' of the press 'from the heart of my bottom'. He explained his antipathy like this: 'I got tired of the press taking what I saw as my best qualities – my determination, my commitment and my dedication – and turning them around. "Determined" became "obsessive", "committed" became "selfish" and so on. I battled that for years.' Faldo, though, was smart enough to know when to shed his crustiness and later he became an affable, even garrulous, television pundit.

TORVILL AND DEAN
1957– AND 1958–

ICE DANCERS Jayne Torvill and Christopher Dean were so good they were not only world and Olympic champions, they made their sport's legendarily unimpressible judges come close to pronouncing them perfect. In defiance of the British tradition of finishing well behind whoever the best Russians were at the time, they set a standard that ice dancers still strive to attain. The pair's dalliance with perfection was at its most electric at the 1984 Winter Olympics in Sarajevo where they won the gold medal with across-the-board 6.0s, the maximum mark, for artistic impression. Their interpretation of Ravel's *Bolero*, which the judges agreed was faultless, solved the problem for millions of Britons of how to become misty-eyed on the night of 14 February. The television audience on that particular St Valentine's Day peaked at 24 million, with even parliament adjourning to allow members to watch. Torvill, an insurance clerk, and Dean, a police cadet, had done passingly well with other partners before they came together in 1975. Different temperamentally, they occasionally clashed off the ice but on it Dean's creative brilliance perfectly complemented Torvill's technical precision. David Wallechinsky, the American chronicler of Olympic Games, reckoned Torvill and Dean brought Nottingham 'more glory than D. H. Lawrence, though not quite as much as Robin Hood'. Early on, the financial support the pair received from their home town – in 1980 Nottingham City Council granted them £14,000 – drew protests. By the end, there was general agreement that the city fathers had rarely invested more wisely. As well as their Olympic gold, they won four successive world titles (1981 to 1984) and – ten years after Sarajevo – took an Olympic bronze at Lillehammer in what was widely seen as an ill-judged comeback. They performed together for the last time in 1998. The social status of their partnership was, for a while, one of the nation's favourite guessing games. Torvill did admit that she had had a crush on Dean, but once that had passed it 'was like a marriage without sex'. Dean took the sex right out of it when he said they were so tied together they were 'almost a brand name'. In the 1990s, they turned away from each other to find their marital partners.

DALEY THOMPSON
1958–

DALEY THOMPSON was an incorrigible exhibitionist who regarded showing off during competition as his reward for the many lonely hours of toil that made him the world's foremost decathlete. He said he trained three times on Christmas Day every year for fifteen years. This entitled him to whistle along with the national anthem when he won his first Olympic gold in 1980 and wear a provocative T-shirt when he won his second in Los Angeles four years later. He taunted his hosts by parading the message '. . . what about the TV coverage', a dig at the jingoism of the US network that televised the Games. He also made headlines in 1982 by uttering an obscenity on live TV after receiving the BBC Sports Personality of the Year award. Thompson, who was born in London, the son of a Nigerian father and Scottish mother, was an irrepressible force forged by a powerful physique and personality. At eighteen, he had sufficiently mastered the ten disciplines to take part in the first of his four Olympic decathlons at the 1976 Games in Montreal. He came eighteenth. In 1980 in Moscow he won the gold. A lesser competitor might have rejoiced that his great rival, the West German Guido Kratschmer, had withdrawn because of a boycott. Thompson sought him out and beat him two months before the Games with a world-record score. The Moscow crowd, parsimonious with their appreciation of foreign athletes, then gave him a standing ovation as he completed the 1500 metres to win the gold medal. In 1983, Thompson added the world championship title to the Olympic, European and Commonwealth crowns he already held. Thompson turned the 1984 Olympic decathlon into a

bravura display of his showman-
ship and all-round proficiency
as an athlete as he saw off
the challenge of the world
record holder, Jürgen
Hingsen of West Germany.
Knowing he had to run the
1500 metres in 4 minutes
34.98 seconds to challenge
Hingsen's record, he pulled a
typically perverse stunt by

easing off to finish two hundredths of a second outside this
time. Two years later, officials corrected his time for the 110
metres hurdles, lowering it by one hundredth of a second, and
credited him with a share of the world record retrospectively.
He went to the 1988 Olympics, but by now injury and age
had blunted his competitive edge and he came fourth. After
retiring from athletics in 1992, he became a fitness coach
across a range of sports, including football and tennis, and a
motivational speaker.

LINFORD CHRISTIE
— 1960– —

LINFORD CHRISTIE had to deal with approbation and imputa-
tion in almost equal measure during his seventeen years in
international athletics. For most of this time he was one of the
world's swiftest runners, unrivalled by British male sprinters,
with twenty-three major championship medals. Two expres-
sions defined Christie: the stare with which he intimidated

opponents and his winning smile once over the line. The sinister look came to represent the dark moments, which included a two-year ban in semi-retirement after he tested positive for the performance-enhancing steroid nandrolone; the smile reflected the pride in his achievements that the British public acknowledged by voting him the BBC sports personality of the year in 1993. Christie protested his innocence over drugs, saying he would take a lie detector test any time. In 2001, a rancorous exchange with Sebastian Coe, who had been a team-mate of Christie's and later received a peerage, revived the drug-taking issue. Coe suggested Christie had been lucky to escape a ban at the 1988 Olympics when the authorities accepted ginseng was the cause of a positive dope test. Christie ascribed 'a racial connotation' to Coe's remarks. Christie came with his family to live in London when he was seven. He dismissed stories of an impoverished childhood in Jamaica – 'We weren't rich but we got along' – which resulted in a rebellious streak that delayed his maturing as an athlete. Even so, he was twenty-eight before he ran in his first Olympics, finishing third in the 100 metres in Seoul in 1988 before being promoted to the silver-medal position when Canada's Ben Johnson was stripped of the gold. Christie kept his medal after the ginseng controversy and at the 1992 Olympics in Barcelona produced his greatest performance, his only sub-10-second run of the year (9.96 seconds), to win the 100-metres gold. At thirty-two, he was the oldest champion for the short sprint. A year later he won gold at the world championships and he went on to defend the 100-metres title at the 1996 Olympics in Atlanta. After being disqualified for two false starts, Christie refused to leave the track, the charitable view of his action being that it was fitting for a proud champion. Christie had a mighty physique, which he exhibited after races by rolling down his running top. His tight Lycra also showed off what a newspaper christened 'Linford's lunchbox', a term that he disliked intensely. When the judge in a libel case asked, 'What is Linford Christie's lunchbox?', Christie replied, 'They are making a reference to my genitals, your honour. I think it's disgusting.'

ELLERY HANLEY
———— 1961– ————

ELLERY HANLEY was occasionally referred to as the Black Pearl but the nickname never stuck; his real name was quite enough. In the 1980s and early 1990s, Ellery was a widely understood word. It meant a presence on a rugby league field that gave off an electric shock of excitement. Hanley accentuated this aura by making few public pronouncements during his playing days. One reason for this was what he regarded as the media's unnecessary obsession with his scrapes with the law when he was young. Hanley was probably the only Great Britain player who would have been an automatic selection for the dominant Australia sides he played against. Although properly admired for being able to play just about anywhere, it was as a loose forward, the position that Wigan's Kiwi coach Graham Lowe adapted to make the most of Hanley's versatility, that he exceeded being merely very good. He was hard, smart, quick-footed, passed well and was an implacable but principled opponent. Playing for Balmain Tigers in the 1988 Grand Final in Australia, he was knocked unconscious when the Canterbury player Terry Lamb caught him with his elbow and he fell awkwardly on his head. Hanley left others to debate whether Lamb took him out on purpose. He said simply that these things happened in a physical game. 'I have no malice towards Lamb, none at all, regardless of the incident being deliberate or accidental.' Hanley, whose parents were from St Kitts, was born in Leeds. He was a good enough footballer to have played the game professionally but chose rugby league, despite never having watched a match, when Bradford Northern made him a good offer in 1978. His best season for Bradford was 1984-5 when over the course of thirty-seven matches he became the first non-winger for seventy years to score more than fifty tries. In 1985, he moved to Wigan for a fee of £150,000 and during his second season scored 63 tries playing at centre, stand-off and loose forward, an all-time record for a player other than a winger. In the late 1980s, when Wigan towered over the English game, Hanley 'was special, the indispensable player', said Maurice Lindsay, who ran the club. He ended his career in England as player-coach at Leeds, where in the 1994-5 season he showed his class was imperishable by reeling off another try-scoring record – 41 being a world best for a forward. He had a brief spell with Western Suburbs in Australia before going back to Balmain in 1996-7. Of his time in Australia, he said: 'I wanted to be respected by the Australians as well, because their game is so superior to ours.'

STEVE REDGRAVE
⟶ 1962– ⟶

IN ROWING, Steve Redgrave found an outlet to satisfy a yearning for achievement that, because of his dyslexia, the classroom never would. Brutally strong and competitive, the builder's son from Marlow in Buckinghamshire was the first male to win gold medals in endurance events at five successive Olympics. His capacity for punishment in the gym was endless – he relished bench-pressing up to 120 kilograms (265 pounds) – and its reward was evident in the final reckoning: four of his five Olympic victories eked out by less than two seconds. He also demonstrated great fortitude by carrying on despite severe colitis and, at his fifth Olympics in 2000, diabetes. Redgrave began rowing at his comprehensive school and he came to refer to the nearby River Thames as the other woman in his life. He won his first Olympic gold in 1984 in the coxed fours on Lake Casitas outside Los Angeles. At the 1988 Olympics in Seoul, he competed in two events with Andy Holmes. Despite there being some grit in this relationship (although not the outright hostility that some claimed), they won gold in the coxless pairs and bronze in the coxed pairs. Atlanta in 1992 saw the start of Redgrave's Olympic successes with Matthew Pinsent, the

BEST OF BRITISH

STEVE REDGRAVE

towering Old Etonian with lungs like bellows, a huge reach and a quiet determination that gelled perfectly with Redgrave's intense drive. With Pinsent perched serenely in the stroke seat and Redgrave heaving and hectoring behind, they were as mighty a combination as rowing has produced. Even Redgrave's wife, Ann, referred to the bonding between these two red-blooded alpha males as a marriage. After they won the coxless pairs for a second time in Barcelona in 1996, Redgrave thought it was time for a divorce. He announced before climbing out of the boat: 'Anyone who sees me go anywhere near a boat again, ever, you've got my permission to shoot me.' Not long after, though, as he contemplated the excitement that the 2000 Games in Sydney would generate, he changed his mind. By the time of those Games he was thirty-eight and feeling the effects of his diabetes. Although he had gained selection to the coxless four on merit, along with Pinsent, Tim Foster and James Cracknell, he admitted later he had considered withdrawing. He said he told the coach, Jürgen Gröbler: 'I'm giving up; I'm not going to make it.' Gröbler talked him round and in a magnificent race, in which they had to repel a frantically fast finish by Italy, the quartet just held on – and after this one Redgrave really had had enough. The knighthood that followed was a formality. In retirement, he raised money for his charitable foundation and, through the sort of diligent application that he brought to his rowing, turned himself into an effective public speaker.

LAURA DAVIES
1963–

LAURA DAVIES, golfer, gambler, racehorse owner and Arsenal and England football fan, combined fun and success in a way few sportsmen or women had managed since professionalism submerged the amateur ethos. In 1994, when she became the first player to win on five different tours, she bypassed the practice range before one of her victories, headed instead for the tennis courts and finished off with an arduous session at the roulette wheel. She disarmed critics of her style, of which there were many, with a smile, a quip and, perhaps, if she were feeling just a tiny bit mean, an invitation to study her record. Or she might simply salute them with a dab of the brakes as she drove off in her Ferrari. She took her cue from the advice she received from her club pro as a young player. He watched her for a while and said: 'Never, ever have a lesson.' Davies, born in Coventry, had a solid if unspectacular amateur career before launching herself on the professional scene in 1985 with as resounding a thwack as she hit one of her tee shots. 'She's the only human I know who, when she's swinging at full tilt, has both feet off the ground as she thumps the ball,' said the golf writer Bill Elliott. (She did finesse too, incidentally.) In her first two years, she headed the European tour's order of merit. She then went to America in 1987 to become the first British winner of the US Open, beating JoAnne Carner and Ayako Okamoto in an 18-hole playoff. Her appearance in the Open forced the LPGA, the North American tour, to change their constitution and grant Davies instant membership. When the tournament commenced, she had, strictly speaking, been ineligible to compete. Davies's domination of the European tour waned when in 1988 she started to divide her time between the European and American tours. She topped the LPGA's prize-money list in 1994, set a record of nineteen eagles on the 2004 tour and over the years won twenty of their titles. She re-established command in Europe by winning the order of merit in 2004 and 2006. One of her few failures was in 2004 when she entered a European men's event, the first woman to do so, and did not make the cut. Davies was a popular and galvanising member of the European team who enjoyed successes in the biennial Solheim Cup against the US. She was the only player from either side to play in the first nine of these contests, her breezy, ram-you-damn-you style bringing a nice contrast to the buttoned-up competitiveness of many of those around her. Her love of football once landed her a fine for watching an England match on a portable TV while playing a tournament.

LENNOX LEWIS
1965–

LENNOX LEWIS grew gradually into as imposing a world heavyweight champion as he was a physical presence. Those who regarded the big man, 6 feet 5 inches and with an enormous 84-inch reach, as a moderate fighter finally changed their minds after he made a wreck of Mike Tyson in June 2002. Up until then, the inconsistency of the middle years of his professional career invited the scepticism with which the fighting press have tended to view all but the very best heavyweights. Lewis's early fights were with other children in

West Ham, east London, where he was born. But the playground scrapper did not develop a desire to be a boxer until much later. Instead, he said, he wanted to be a fireman. He and his mother, Violet, emigrated to Canada when he was twelve and it was here that Lewis turned into an outstanding amateur. Boxing for Canada, he won the 1988 Olympic super-heavyweight title when, despite having a broken thumb, he stopped the American Riddick Bowe. Lewis restored his allegiance to Britain when he turned professional in 1989. He knocked out 17 of his first 20 opponents, but his rise to the world title in 1993 came by default when Bowe, by now undisputed world heavyweight champion, again featured prominently in his life. Bowe held a press conference at which he dumped his WBC championship belt into a bin rather than fight Lewis with a result that the title was awarded to the British fighter. In 1994, Lewis suffered an unexpected setback when knocked out by Oliver McCall with a devastating punch that few saw coming, least of all the recipient. In a bizarre rematch in 1997, McCall, who had a substance-abuse problem, stopped fighting, burst into tears and left the referee with no option but to stop the fight. Lewis had other dramatic confrontations, notably with Evander Holyfield, the first of their two fights scandalously being scored a draw even though the punch count was 348–130 to Lewis, and with Hasim Rahman, who knocked Lewis out before being flattened himself in the rematch. The Tyson fight generated huge interest despite Tyson's best fighting days having passed. The bout grossed an unprecedented $103 million in pay-per-view television rights alone. Lewis won it easily, jabbing Tyson into a hopeless position before knocking him out. Lewis weighed in at a career-high 256 pounds for his last fight in 2003 and, although generally unimpressive, landed some brutal punches to stop Vitali Klitschko. The facial damage suffered by Klitschko needed 63 stitches to put right. Lewis, who was his own man and refused to be lured into the clutches of the acquisitive promoter Don King, showed a social conscience when he opened the Lennox Lewis College in east London to create opportunities for young black people. It closed down because of funding difficulties.

RED RUM
1965–1995

RED RUM was unrivalled at clearing obstacles, of which he encountered many: a difficult upbringing after he was born to an oddball – crazy, some called her – mother; being mistakenly classified as a sprinter; a serious foot disease; being rejected constantly by trainers and those pundits who dismissed his first Grand National victory; and, above all, Aintree's tyrannous jumps in the days before they were made less intimidating. He survived to become as big a celebrity as any biped because, as one of his biographers put it, he possessed 'more toughness, more resilience, more downright soaring courage than any horse I've been privileged to know'. Aintree was where Red Rum ran his first race at the start of a modest flat-racing career in 1967. It was the steeplechase course that would transform him. Course and horse combined for their first Grand National in 1973. By then, the bay gelding had been through four trainers and been sent by his octogenarian owner, Noel le Mare, to a fifth. This was the former taxi driver Ginger McCain, who trained his horses on the sands of

Southport. McCain also took Red Rum for therapeutic swims in the sea before each National. In 1973, at his first National, Red Rum seemed as out of it as all the other horses when the top weight, Crisp, charged clear by at least twenty lengths at Becher's second time round. In the end, though, Crisp succumbed to the handicapper's draconian burden as Red Rum got up to win by less than a length in record time. It might have been remembered simply as the race Crisp lost if had it not transpired that it was the

BEST OF BRITISH

RED RUM

start of Red Rum's very special relationship with the most treacherous obstacle course in sport. He would finish with an unrivalled National record of three wins and two seconds in five runs in successive years. After Red Rum won again in 1974, he suffered defeat the following year. Some blamed Brian Fletcher, one of twenty jockeys who rode him, for delaying too long. Fletcher lost the ride in 1976 when, with Tommy Stack on board, Red Rum was second again, held off by Rag Trade. Stack retained the ride in 1977 and this time they destroyed the field. At the age of twelve, Rummie was considered too old by some to take on the big fences but he finished, ears pricked, 25 lengths in front and with the crowd creating a din more fervid than any previously heard at Aintree. Red Rum lived for a further eighteen years and at his many public appearances seemed as conscious as those who milled around him that he had done something out of the ordinary. He was buried at the Aintree finishing line.

PAUL GASCOIGNE
1967–

PAUL GASCOIGNE left the world wondering whether, by playing the savant idiot, he had fulfilled or squandered his potential as a footballer. There was enough evidence from his schooldays that, contrary to the England manager Bobby Robson's observation, Gascoigne was much cleverer than a brush. For whatever reason, though, he often turned to acting the fool – mainly a harmless one, but not always – which may have barred him from becoming an unimaginably good player. Conversely, it may have assisted him in salvaging so many brilliant performances by freeing his mind from the inner demons that led him to bouts of drinking and drug abuse. At its most enchanted, notably during the 1990 World Cup, his football was captivating. It was hardly possible to believe he was the same player when he performed ludicrously in the 1991 FA Cup final for Tottenham against Nottingham Forest and ended up severely injuring himself rather than the opponents he chased so dementedly. Gascoigne grew up in unpromising surroundings in Tyneside. An incident when he saw a friend killed by a car, and a serious illness suffered by his father had a detrimental effect. As a result, football became a fragile refuge rather than the solid core of his life. He signed for Newcastle United in 1983 and made his League debut in 1985. In 1988, he moved to Tottenham for a record £2.2 million with a growing reputation as a strong and clever midfield player. He could confound opponents with his acceleration and close control, open up defences with the originality of his passing and score thrilling goals. He was an inspirational contributor to England's run to the 1990 World Cup semi-final, in which they lost to West Germany. In that match, Gascoigne burst into tears when he received a yellow card that would have kept him out of the final had England qualified. The melodramatic episode is often given as the starting point of the boom that would transform English football, but Gascoigne's decision to recall it by crying copiously in a TV ad selling crisps illustrated the less positive effect it had on him. He seemed to be convinced it was now compulsory to behave in a puerile manner whenever possible. Even so, he revived his career at Rangers after an unproductive time with Lazio in Italy. At Euro 96, he reminded the world both how good and silly he was with a brilliant goal against Scotland that he celebrated by miming a drunken incident in which he was involved before the tournament. His days as an international ended bitterly when Glenn Hoddle omitted him from his final selection for the 1998 World Cup in France. Gascoigne responded by wrecking a hotel room. The rest of his career, like George Best's before him, was a steady progression from bad to worse, the low point of which was a ridiculous move to China that lasted for just four games.

KELLY HOLMES
——— 1970– ———

KELLY HOLMES was one of the best young lorry drivers in the British Army before she returned to athletics to become the best female middle-distance runner in the world. Her two wins at the 2004 Olympics made her the first British woman to claim more than one gold medal at the same Games. Holmes's success was based on a proclivity for hard work in training that grew even more demonic whenever there were male runners to be left in her slipstream. Her gong tally – three Olympic medals (she had won a bronze at the 2000 Games), four at world championships, two at European championships and three at Commonwealth Games – would have been many more but for her spell in the Army and injuries that affected her for seven years. Holmes was born in Pembury, Kent, the daughter of Derrick Holmes, a Jamaican-born car mechanic, and an English mother, Pam Norman. Her talent for running soon revealed itself. After joining Tonbridge Athletics Club at the age of twelve, she won the English schools 1500 metres in her second season. When she joined the Army at eighteen, she abandoned athletics to drive heavy-duty trucks. After her corps was disbanded, she became a physical training instructor, reaching the rank of sergeant. An Army athletics coach suggested she return to the sport, but she said later: 'I wasn't sure. I was enjoying life being completely army barmy.' What persuaded her to resume competitive running was seeing an athlete she had beaten before her Army days taking part at the 1992 Olympics. She soon won national titles at 800 and 1500 metres but success at the big international events was limited by a range of ailments, including a stress fracture, a ruptured Achilles tendon and a viral illness. In 2003, she suffered a succession of leg injuries, which, she later told a newspaper, led to depression that caused her to self-harm and, on at least one occasion, consider suicide. She recovered in time for the 2004 Olympics in Athens, running six races in nine days to carry off first the 800-metres and then the 1500-metres titles. At the age of thirty-four, she ran perfectly judged finals to subdue the impressive defending champion Maria Mutola over two laps and sort out three Russians ganging up against her over the longer distance. Each time she dropped towards the back of the field before using her strength and unbreakable will to grind down the opposition with a run for home from about 300 metres. Her victories, she said, brought to an end 'twenty years of dreaming'. She was made a Dame Commander of the Order of the British Empire in the 2005 New Year's Honours List.

MARTIN JOHNSON
⟶ 1970– ⟵

MARTIN JOHNSON set an example that manly Englishmen had once looked for in their military commanders. His leadership of the England team who won the 2003 Rugby World Cup in Australia was of the granite-jawed, unblinking, do-what-I-do-because-I-don't-say-much variety that meant his men went willingly with him in to ruck, maul and brawl. He grew increasingly terse and determined as the moment of his greatest triumph approached. When England lined up in the wrong place before they beat Ireland at Lansdowne Road in the 2003

Six Nations, Johnson refused to reposition his team, which meant the President of Ireland had to walk on the turf, not on the carpet. While outrage and apologies swirled in the background, Johnson referred to 'a fuss about nothing'. On the successful tour to New Zealand that followed, sin-binnings left England with a six-man scrum against the All Blacks, to which Johnson responded with the exhortation: 'Get down and shove.' Asked what went through his head as he packed down, Johnson said: 'My spine.' A physically imposing second-row forward, Johnson liked nothing more than a hard forward battle. A favourite match was against Ireland in 1995. 'We played into a gale-force wind for forty minutes and came off two tries to nil up. The backs never had the ball all game. It was all the forwards. Fantastic. Quality rugby.' Johnson, who was born in Solihull, might have ended up playing for the All Blacks. A 1989 trip to New Zealand to further his rugby education resulted in his touring Australia with the All Blacks under-21 side in 1990. His New Zealand girlfriend saved the situation by marrying him and saying she wanted to settle in England. He duly returned to make his international debut in a 16–15 win over France at Twickenham in 1993. Apart from an incident in 2000, when he came close to leading a strike by England players over pay, the only bad publicity Johnson received with the national team was when he lost his temper on the field, which was not infrequently. He played for England for eleven years, went on three Lions tours, two as captain, and was a stalwart of outstanding Leicester sides. All his many achievements were overshadowed by the events of 22 November 2003 when England beat Australia 20–17 in Sydney to win the World Cup. After leading the team superbly, it was Johnson, one of the few still in command of his wits, who drove play to within kicking distance of the posts so that Jonny Wilkinson could drop the winning goal seconds from the end of extra time.

TONY McCOY
1974–

TONY McCOY, known simply by his initials AP in the horseracing world, turned jump racing into his personal fiefdom. He lost none of his fervour once he established that he could churn out victories with extraordinary regularity, regardless of having to share the responsibility for his success with 1,000-pound animals performing perilous feats of athleticism. In addition to the monotony of winning, McCoy, who at close to 5 feet 11 inches was very tall for a jockey, had his resolve tested by a constant battle with the scales. Trainer Colm Murphy said of McCoy after he rode Brave Inca to victory in the 2006 Champion Hurdle at Cheltenham: 'He's as tough as old nails and he'd probably ride if he had no legs and no arms. I think he and Brave Inca are a match made in heaven. One is tough and the other is tougher but I don't know which is which.' McCoy, born in Moneyglass, County Antrim, rode his first winner as a seventeen-year-old before moving to England in 1994. It took only until 1995–6 for him to become champion jump jockey, driving home his mounts with a physical riding method that stood out amid the less frantic styles of most of his main rivals. For the next ten years and more, he held on to the title, laying waste countless records along the way. In 2001–2 he rode 289 winners, beating Sir Gordon Richards's 269, which had stood since 1947 as a record for all racing, flat and National Hunt. His devotion to winning was so overwhelming that he declared the following season a disaster because he failed to register a further improvement. Evidence of McCoy's toughness was plentiful. He secured his ninth title by keeping his absences from the track to a minimum after breaking an arm and crushing a cheekbone. At Cheltenham one day his mount fell on the flat, smashing his teeth. The blood and gore were enough to make spectators retch. There was even an appeal over the public address system for a dentist. McCoy cleaned himself up, ignored the pain and rode the winner of the last. 'My face could have been broken to bits,' he said, 'but I would have still come out to ride that horse. He has a great attitude to life.' Out of the saddle, he is a charming and approachable man.

ELLEN MACARTHUR
——— 1976– ———

ELLEN MACARTHUR met most of the criteria that might have been expected to disqualify her from her greatest seafaring triumph. Small, emotional and not long recovered from illness, possessing limited experience and from one of England's landlocked counties, MacArthur took on the world's oceans during the winter of 2004–5. In just over 71 days, she completed a solo circumnavigation of the globe in a time that broke the record by more than a day. Some critics sought to belittle her effort on the grounds of the technology she used. They did so from comfortable, centrally heated homes. On the gender issue, the American balloonist, sailor and aviator Steve Fossett boldly went where other commentators felt too timid to venture. 'I counted three times when she cried amid the extreme workload and pressure – unmistakably a woman in every respect,' said Fossett, who based his appreciation of MacArthur on filmed extracts of her second-place finish in another round-the-world challenge, the 2001 Vendée Globe. MacArthur, the daughter of teachers from Whatstandwell, Derbyshire, developed a fascination for sailing from reading books such as *Swallows and Amazons* and trips to the seaside with an aunt. She saved her school dinner money to buy her first boat and, aged eighteen, sailed solo around Britain. While recovering from the glandular illness mononucleosis, she decided to devote herself to sailing. MacArthur based herself in a small shed in a boatyard and wrote begging letters for sponsorship. While the replies trickled in – two in response to 2,500 letters sent out – she prepared herself for what she hoped lay ahead. The British firm Kingfisher provided her with the financial break she needed. It was in the boat bearing that company's name that she grabbed the attention of seafarer and landlubber when she raced home second in the Vendée Globe. Millions watched telecasts of her doing repair work at the top of a 27-metre mast as it swooped and swayed in Atlantic gales and delivering tearful messages from her cabin. Her attempt on the round-the-world record in *B&Q Castorama* that began on 28 November 2004 became a national event. Her time at the finishing line on 7 February 2005 was 71 days 14 hours 18 minutes 3 seconds; one day 8 hours 35 minutes 49 seconds inside the record. As with the sailing Francises, Drake (1580) and Chichester (1967), who were also recognised by Queen Elizabeths, MacArthur's decoration – she was elevated to Dame Commander of the Order of the British Empire – was announced in her moment of triumph rather than being delayed until the next honours list.

JONNY WILKINSON
1979–

JONNY WILKINSON made moments of static contemplation as important a part of a rugby union match as the all-action mayhem that predominated. The England fly-half's preparatory freeze, with hands cupped in front of him while he sagged slightly at the knees, transformed place-kicking into something approaching an exact science. Even when kicking out of hand in open play, and with opponents reaching out to drag him down, Wilkinson would conjure an instant's composure before swinging his boot. Never was this more thrillingly executed than when he drop-kicked the goal, with his supposedly less reliable right foot, that won the 2003 World Cup 27 seconds before the end of extra time in Sydney. 'We had Wilko in front of the sticks to win the World Cup – and you just wouldn't have anyone else there, would you?' his captain Martin Johnson asked, rhetorically. In the UK, a TV audience of 15 million, a record for a rugby match, watched as Wilkinson's kick sailed between the posts. He had already landed four penalties, one of them a 47-metre monster, as he contributed 15 points to England's 20–17 final win over Australia. Wilkinson was what the English, if not everyone else, liked to think of as the archetypal young Englishman. He was good looking, muscular, assiduous, modest, polite and gifted. Born in Frimley, Hampshire, he became, at eighteen years 301 days, England's youngest capped international for seventy-one years when he came on for the final few minutes of the Five Nations match against Ireland in April 1998. The following season he played throughout the Five Nations at centre, his 22 successful kicks signalling England now had a reliable source of points. In those matches, he showed all the other attributes that would help establish him at fly-half: a strong pass off either hand, a deceptive change of pace, even if his top speed was modest, and a tackle whose severity was out of all proportion to his size. This last virtue turned out also to be a flaw because it exposed a congenital weakness in his spine and contributed to a string of injuries that limited his activity after the World Cup victory. Although he made a second Lions tour in 2005, he did not play again for England after the 2003 World Cup until the 2007 Six Nations. Typically, though, he announced his return with a record-breaking performance, 27 points in England's 42–20 win over Scotland, as he surged further ahead as his country's leading points scorer.

BEST OF BRITISH

JONNY WILKINSON

The list of fellow journos and authors, some of them sadly departed, and many others whose help I have solicited or whose work or knowledge has been an invaluable source of reference is almost as long as the number of heroes. Here goes with trying to name you all:

Michael Aylwin, Pat Butcher, Mick Collins, Philip Cornwall, Bill Elliott, Carolly Erickson, David Foot, Reg Gadney, Brian Glanville, Phyllis Grosskurth, Norman Harris, J. C. Holt, Steve Hutchings, Jamie Jackson, Peter Jackson, Alan Little, Vic Marks, Kevin Mitchell, Chris Nawat, Brian Oliver, Oliver Owen, Steve Parry, Jim Parsons, Nick Pitt, Peter Radford, Dudley Savill, Brough Scott, Greg Struthers, Michael Tanner, David Terry, John Thicknesse, Clem and Greg Thomas, JBG Thomas, Daniel Topolski, Nick Townsend, Brian Vine, David Wallechinsky, Paul Wilson, John Woodcock.

To those I have missed: you know who you are and the thanks are just as heartfelt . . .

Tristan Jones deserves a special mention for engaging me for the project and then disengaging me for the project and then disengaging me from all the solecisms and other crimes comitted in the original text.

Reference books I used extensively included: *1966 Almanack of Sport*, *Barclays World of Cricket*, *The Boxing Register*, *Encyclopaedia of Sport* (1897, Vols I & II), *The Encyclopaedia of Tennis*, *The Oxford Companion to Sports and Games*, *The Sunday Times 1000 Makers of Sport*, *The Wisden Book of Obituaries* and *Wisden Cricketers' Almanack* (various).

The list of fellow journos and authors, some of them sadly departed, and many others whose help I have solicited or whose work or knowledge has been an invaluable source of reference is almost as long as the number of heroes. Here goes with trying to name you all:

Michael Aylwin, Pat Butcher, Mick Collins, Philip Cornwall, Bill Elliott, Carolly Erickson, David Foot, Reg Gadney, Brian Glanville, Phyllis Grosskurth, Norman Harris, J. C. Holt, Steve Hutchings, Jamie Jackson, Peter Jackson, Alan Little, Vic Marks, Kevin Mitchell, Chris Nawat, Brian Oliver, Oliver Owen, Steve Parry, Jim Parsons, Nick Pitt, Peter Radford, Dudley Savill, Brough Scott, Greg Struthers, Michael Tanner, David Terry, John Thicknesse, Clem and Greg Thomas, JBG Thomas, Daniel Topolski, Nick Townsend, Brian Vine, David Wallechinsky, Paul Wilson, John Woodcock.

To those I have missed: you know who you are and the thanks are just as heartfelt . . .

Tristan Jones deserves a special mention for engaging me for the project and then disengaging me for the project and then disengaging me from all the solecisms and other crimes comitted in the original text.

Reference books I used extensively included: *1966 Almanack of Sport, Barclays World of Cricket, The Boxing Register, Encyclopaedia of Sport* (1897, Vols I & II), *The Encyclopaedia of Tennis, The Oxford Companion to Sports and Games, The Sunday Times 1000 Makers of Sport, The Wisden Book of Obituaries* and *Wisden Cricketers' Almanack* (various).

reliable source of points. In those matches, he showed all the other attributes that would help establish him at fly-half: a strong pass off either hand, a deceptive change of pace, even if his top speed was modest, and a tackle whose severity was out of all proportion to his size. This last virtue turned out also to be a flaw because it exposed a congenital weakness in his spine and contributed to a string of injuries that limited his activity after the World Cup victory. Although he made a second Lions tour in 2005, he did not play again for England after the 2003 World Cup until the 2007 Six Nations. Typically, though, he announced his return with a record-breaking performance, 27 points in England's 42–20 win over Scotland, as he surged further ahead as his country's leading points scorer.

BEST OF BRITISH

JONNY WILKINSON

INDEX